TRUST
IS THE NEW
CURRENCY

How to build trust, attract the right
partners and create wealth through
business and investments

SHEILA HOLT
FREDRIK SANDVALL

Praise

'*Trust is the New Currency* is a much-needed book in this fast-moving world. If every business learned to create a profound sense of trust through everything they do, not only would their bottom line improve but it would create a culture that attracts great talent and opportunities. Consciously creating trust is good for business, good for people and good for the world.'
— Masami Sato, Founder, B1G1

'Trust is more important than ever. This book offers a model for entrepreneurs to create the foundations of trust faster and to enjoy the process. Sheila and Fredrik draw upon their long and varied experiences as entrepreneurs and the lessons they've gained in building trust. This jargon-free book will give you practical wisdom for building stronger bonds around your business and brand.'
— Daniel Priestley, CEO, Dent Global

'A fantastic, straightforward and honest book. It highlights the importance of having a higher purpose or, as the authors call it, the big why, which we as entrepreneurs can use as rocket fuel for the greater good.'
— Mike Frisby, Multiple Property Business Owner

'I love the concept of this book and I agree that "trust is the new currency". This book has been well thought out and presented in an easy to understand format, which will help you to build an effective core team. All entrepreneurs can use the high-level information here to introduce trust and keep it flowing within their business. It's great to see Sheila and Fredrik collaborate in this way. Highly recommended.'

— Simon Zutshi, Author of bestseller *Property Magic* and Founder of Property Investors Network

'Trust is the new currency. Couldn't have put it better myself. In the modern world of business, the internet and social media, trust is one of the most important, yet overlooked, tools. By applying the principles that the authors detail in this book within your business, communication and relationships will improve, you'll be able to manage projects better and will find it easier to get the results you want.'

— Rob Wilkinson, Co-founder, Crowd with Us

'Three new models explained simply and with clarity. The Trust Triangle, the Business Engine and the Investment Triangle are bound to help any entrepreneur on their journey to success. Apply them in your business.'

— Andrew Eggelton, Presenting Mentor

R3THINK PRESS

First published in Great Britain 2019
by Rethink Press (www.rethinkpress.com)

Cover image © Vaclav Krivsky | Shutterstock

With gratitude to everyone we have worked with over the years who has made us into who we are today.

To my family: Harriet, Ivan and Charlie Sandvall.

Contents

Foreword

Success and failure are both very predictable.

In today's market, where small businesses are starved of finance, large businesses are falling like dominoes and the high-street banks will only lend to you if you can prove you don't need the money, have you ever stopped to question how the market-leading entrepreneurs of today are breaking away from the pack, have access to more capital than they know what to do with and are using the unique opportunities available at this time to thrive?

Success and failure are both very predictable and, through reading this book, you will gain insight into the models and methods used by some of the world's leading entrepreneurs, as they observe the masses – and do the opposite.

I have been an entrepreneur all my life and having met, trained, partnered and worked with thousands of professionals from around the world, I can say that the authors of this book are two I highly recommend and trust to write authoritatively on this topic, and whom I hold in high personal regard.

I first met Sheila and Fredrik at one of our Property Entrepreneur training events back in 2014. Clients from around the world come to these events to learn about the core competencies and fundamentals required in starting, systemising and scaling businesses in today's market. Three of those elements that need to be mastered are 'profile', 'finance' and 'team' and, once I had spent time with Sheila and Fredrik independently, I provided a connection, as I felt that collaboratively, they could combine these to become a force to be reckoned with.

The rest is history.

Business and investments are a lifelong craft to be mastered and if you follow the teachings of this book, whilst you will not get rich quickly, I can assure you that you will get wealthy well.

Success in this space is highly strategic and, over the coming pages and chapters, you will gain the required insight into the true value that is now placed on people over paperwork in the world of business and finance today, as well as how to magnetise your business and your position to capitalise on this.

Internally, you need to attract talent and, through reading this book, you will learn the power of mastering profiles, looking for complementary skill sets and, much like Sheila and Fredrik, the art of building the dream team.

The reality is, none of this happens overnight, but my advice is for you to take the decades of wisdom and expertise shared within this book, to grab the quick wins, adopt the philosophies, introduce the methods and models, and then play the long game.

Success and failure are both very predictable. If you can use the direction provided over the sixteen chapters of this book to master what to do, when to do it and who to do it with, you will break away from the pack, as you build trust, attract the right partners and create wealth through business and investments.

It's all a game. Enjoy the journey.

Daniel Hill
Chairman at PPN UK
Entrepreneur of the Year 2018
www.PPN.co.uk

Introduction

These are incredible entrepreneurial times. The number of opportunities available and the speed of technology, as well as innovation, potential support and access to money, are just some of the reasons why these times are so amazing. There is a new currency – trust – and this book will help you understand that trust is invaluable in your business and in your personal growth. You will get insights about how to build trust, attract the right partners and create wealth through business and investments. There is more money available than ever before and you will see clearly that *money follows trust*.

Very few business books have been written about building trust. When trust is talked about, it's usually in the context of how to use it and the value of that trust. This book is about how to *build* trust from scratch rather than repair trust after it has been broken. We are part of an emerging economy in which entrepreneurs create new ways to find money. The core of this new economy is trust.

Increasingly, businesses and entrepreneurs are more aware of their relationships with funders, backers, sponsors and investors, and are openly talking about building trusted relationships. Businesses today use innovative ways to obtain the funding they require for growth and expansion. The world has moved on from the information age to the relationship age, in which businesses are building more transparent and open connections between themselves and their customers. Entrepreneurs are making stronger efforts when it comes to building and relating to their tribes and communities.

Trust is central to the way we operate in our own businesses. We spend time building lifelong relationships. Trust is about facing and serving your customers and is a feeling and an experience, rather than a rational checklist.

Trust is precious and is something money cannot buy. However, money does follow trust. Trust is your ultimate tool to gain more customers, more choice, more wealth and, with that, more freedom.

What you'll discover in this book

The book is divided into three parts. For each part, we've developed a model depicted by a graphic to visually represent its key elements.

Part One: The Foundations Of Trust

This part covers how to reach total trust, which is at the heart of our model. It includes how to establish trust more quickly and using your gut instinct to support your decisions.

- Create trust and place it at the heart of all your business relationships

- Build total trust through the three cornerstones: tuned in, third party and time

- Understand that money follows trust

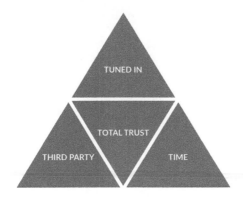

The Trust Triangle

Part Two: Building The Business Engine

This part covers the key roles in the Business Engine.

- Know that the three key roles in any Business Engine are trailblazer, dealmaker and specialist, and each is supported by doers

- Understand where you fit in your own Business Engine and who else you need to add

- Understand how each of these key roles works independently and interdependently to contribute to, and scale, your business

The Business Engine

Part Three: Partnering To Create Wealth Through Business And Investments

This part brings it all together – the powerful combination of purpose, people and project will give you the results you desire.

- Find your purpose, your big why, which is greater than your business

- Understand how each component in the Investment Triangle plays a vital role in the development of any business and the creation of wealth

- Discover that when you're doing things right, you can reach peak performance

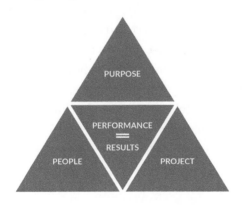

The Investment Triangle

The shape of each of our models is triangular because the triangle is the strongest structure of all. A triangle is impossible to collapse. As a result, it forms the basis of many structures, from bridges and roofs to buildings and pyramids.

When you have three legs to stand on you're sturdy, solid and balanced. Triangular shapes can stand alone, proud and complete, or they can tessellate and create other solid, sturdy shapes with no spaces or gaps in between – no weaknesses.

The Trust Triangle, the Business Engine and the Investment Triangle are standalone models. Each can be used in total isolation and will work well as a complete, independent model. The models can also be used sequentially, in the order we introduce them in the book, or concurrently, in any order. No matter how you use these models, they'll work. Our experiences with people, both in business and through coaching, have led us to create and develop these three models, which we continue to use to grow our own businesses.

Why have you, as an entrepreneur, picked up this book?

It could be any number of reasons:

1. You want to develop a fresh approach to business

2. You want to learn how to build relationships, in your existing or new business, founded on trust

3. You're curious about how to use trust as currency to attract the right business partners

4. You've built a successful business and are now looking for new alliances and investments to create wealth

5. Someone you trust recommended this book

Whatever has attracted you to our book, trust your instincts and enjoy.

Why we've written this book

Fredrik is the dealmaker in Sapphire Lending, Sheila's business, and is therefore a key member of Sheila's Business Engine. We both operate from a basis of trust. Each of us has a range of business experiences and a mountain of people and relationship knowledge. We're both entrepreneurs. Fredrik is passionate about educating others and helping them grow, whilst Sheila is passionate about relationships and how people think. Sheila has her own unique, disruptive way of thinking and doing things. We're both outliers. In other words, our ideas and actions sit outside the bell curve.

We thought it would be fun and challenging to share ideas and add our thoughts to the world, especially those on the topic close to our hearts – relationships built on trust – which underpins how we've built our individual businesses. We offer something fresh, new and maybe even a little thought-provoking about trust and its central position in the world of business today. We both know that money follows trust and that trust can be used in a positive way to create wealth.

To learn more about us and our experience, see the Authors section at the back of the book.

PART ONE
THE FOUNDATIONS OF TRUST

In this first part, you'll discover how trust is built and won and how money follows trust.

1
The Trust Triangle

Society used to simply trust in money. Then the global banking system almost collapsed after the financial crisis of 2007–2008 and universal trust in money wavered. The phrase 'in money we trust' was once the glue that held societies together. Now it no longer holds true because once trust in the financial institutions was lost, economically, countries faltered. Businesses, entrepreneurs and most people suffered because trust in the banks was seriously undermined.

A bank's ability to pay out money on demand, to manage deposits honestly and to put customers' interests before their own was (and still is) at the heart of the public's trust in money. After the financial crisis, the banks started being regarded as faceless organisations in which nobody was held to account;

this made things difficult for entrepreneurs and business people. Entrepreneurs had relied on credit and loans to help their businesses develop and flourish and, because the banks were a primary source of that money, many were forced to close their operations or cut them back massively. As a result, numerous entrepreneurs were left high and dry and feeling let down. The trust that had existed between businesses and financial institutions was lost.

Today, entrepreneurs pursue ways to solve their own challenges – this includes finding alternative sources of finance (peer-to-peer lending or crowdfunding, for example). This new way of thinking about and doing business is grounded in trusted relationships and partnerships. At the beginning of the financial crisis in 2007–2008, business owners began to approach wealthy individuals who wanted their money to work for them and were, therefore, keen to meet entrepreneurs who needed to borrow in order to build their businesses. It's a practice that's on the rise. The financial world is changing beyond all recognition; a new relationship has started to form between money and trust. No longer do we automatically trust in money. Instead, trust is the new currency, and money follows that trust. As an alternative to trading anonymously with banks, entrepreneurs are forming teams of individuals. Total trust is at the centre of these teams and at the core of what we call the Trust Triangle:

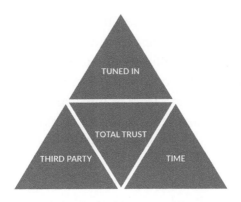

The Trust Triangle

Total trust is in the centre of the Trust Triangle. The three corners of this triangle lead to total trust. The corners are:

- Tuned in – you're tuned in to your instincts, your gut, and you're tuned in to others

- Third party – people refer and recommend you to other people, companies, products or services

- Time – people decide to trust you based on their experience of you over a period of time

Each corner of the triangle in itself builds trust. All three together give you total trust.

The Trust Tringle forms the core of Part One of this book and was developed as a result of Sheila's neuro-linguistic programming background, our combined training and coaching experience as well as observing people. It lies at the centre of our business practices and provides a solid foundation to inform decision-making, allowing us to select ventures and opportunities to work with (covered in Part Three). We put people and trust at the heart of our business and build remarkable teams, covered in Part Two, with whom we have already established total trust.

Trust is part of our daily lives, whether we're aware of it or not. It helps us select whom we work with, partner with and rely on. You are hardwired to trust your instincts and to be tuned in to them. As an entrepreneur, you face many decisions regarding hiring, developing, growing, marketing and pitching. In all these activities, you're both looking for and demonstrating trust.

Why we use the triangle as our model

The triangle is the strongest structure in the world. It cannot collapse – it's mathematically impossible. Isn't that a good place for any business to start? Think back to the pyramids. Even today, design engineers continue to use the triangle as their shape of choice. If you look at building structures, you'll begin to see triangles and patterns of triangles all around you, from the bases of bridges to the roof on your house. When triangles are put together, they tessellate, leaving no space between them, so all sorts of different patterns can be built from one basic triangle. You can also observe triangles if you pay attention to your surroundings in nature.

When you look at the Trust Triangle, you will see something that is strong and firm. It's a building block to which you can attach other triangles – the teams that you build around you. It's a structure that you can grow. The triangle, therefore, represents power and empowerment, and both can lead to total trust.

Let's look at the three corners. The corners of the Trust Triangle work alone as well as together.

Tuned in – Be tuned in to your gut instinct, whatever it's telling you. Also be aware of whether you're tuned in to the person you're considering doing business with. Be attentive to the other person. Listen to their language and what they say. You might need to spend more time getting to know them and the way they think to see if you're compatible or complement each other (see Chapter Two).

Third party – When someone you already trust refers you to other people or businesses, there is implicit trust. Third-party referrals help to speed up the growth and development of your company (see Chapter Three).

Time – Some people build trust over a period of time by observing a person or business, reading about them, meeting them or reading things they've written.

There is no time limit when it comes to building trust (see Chapter Four).

In our businesses we use these three approaches to build total trust. Our Trust Triangle is the basis of the new economy. Use this model as a lens through which to see clearly. By using it, you will transform the way you do business with other people and how they do business with you.

2
Tuned In

Tuning in to people is where *we* start with trust. Both of us intuitively trust people until they prove they can't be trusted, and that's how we work – from an intuitive foundation in business and an intuitive foundation in life. In this chapter, we outline six basic principles that we follow in our own business practices. When put together they interlink, inform and offer insight into how you can:

- Tune in to you

- Follow your gut instinct

- Trust your inner knowledge

For us, it begins with following our gut instinct.

Follow your gut instinct

Following your gut and trusting your inner knowledge is you, as an individual, tuning in to yourself. Some people ignore the guidance of their gut feeling and often, with hindsight, they think, 'I knew I should have followed my instinct.'

Having coached numerous clients over the years, we've seen how some people lack the courage to follow their gut instinct. Although they know instinctively what feels right, they make a decision with their head and follow it. Usually, this works out less in their favour. We advocate tuning in to and trusting your inner knowledge. Doing so also enables you to tune in to other people to help you make decisions about everything in life – and in business.

For example, when buying a home, which is one of the biggest purchases you'll ever make, you might have a checklist of what you're looking for. However, if the home feels good and you can imagine yourself living there, that often means the choice is made. Checklist or no checklist, your inner knowledge has made the decision. Our gut instinct is very much connected with our emotions. Emotions often override logic in decision-making.

Perhaps if we learned from animals, we might trust our gut instincts more. It was widely reported that in advance of the Boxing Day 2004 tsunami in the Indian

Ocean, hours before anybody knew what was to come, animals grazing on low ground suddenly began to flee to higher ground. There was no obvious reason for this, and it seemed perplexing at the time. The weather was calm and the ocean was normal, and yet the animals displayed this erratic behaviour. In fact, the animals were acting on their instincts – their gut reactions – which were telling them to flee from the approaching danger not yet apparent to the human senses. In Sri Lanka alone, over 35,000 people lost their lives when the tsunami struck.[1] It's also reported that no wild animals died.

Meet people how they want to be met

We believe there is much truth in the golden rule: treat other people as you'd like to be treated. We also like to be curious about people, to learn what makes them tick.

Beginning a new business relationship with an open and curious mind (backed up by being our authentic selves) allows us to discover so much more about the other person in terms of social cues and intangibles. These are things we can't see but can feel, such as energy levels and enthusiasm. By being attentive to how the other person is behaving, or appears to us, we can in turn adjust the way we communicate,

---

1   As reported by ABC News (2014) 'Boxing Day Tsunami: How the disaster unfolded 10 years ago', www.abc.net.au/news/2014-12-24/boxing-day-tsunami-how-the-disaster-unfolded/5977568

which helps us to be more 'liked'. After all, it's good to be liked. Adjusting the way we communicate also shows that we're tuning in to the other person. It's about being able to get along in a fruitful business relationship.

Another way to tune in to people is through body language. Pay attention to how they stand, move and breathe, for example. Noticing the total person will give you a story that's more complete than the one they're consciously telling you. As human beings, we are whole systems. We are more than just the words we say. We are also the bodies we live in and how we use those bodies. Let's return to the breathing example. Breathing, which is fundamental to life, offers an opportunity to understand another person on a deeper level. Notice how others are breathing: shallow or deep; fast or slow. Shallow or fast breathing might indicate they're anxious, even if the words they're using make them sound confident. Notice the rhythm of their breath. You may even match the way they're breathing at one point or another. This will give you massive insight into that person and help you build your relationship with them.

Listen

It's important to listen – *really* listen – to the other person without thinking about what you're going to say. Listen to the words they're using to convey their message. Are these words positive or negative? Do they directly express something or merely imply something? Are the words about the speaker or do they refer to other people? Also, be aware of the tone being used to convey the words. Tonality gives many clues about what a person really means.

The other side of listening is hearing what has been missed out and unspoken, as this is also very informative. Tuning in to the unspoken can give you clues and help you understand the subtext or context of a person's message.

Use questions as a tool to create understanding

With over twenty-five years of combined experience in coaching clients, it's apparent that many people in life are afraid to ask specific questions, especially if the topic being discussed is not immediately obvious. Often people will nod and pretend to understand the subject being discussed rather than asking, 'What exactly are you talking about?' or 'What is *it* that you're referring to?' If you're met with a lack of response or a vague or even evasive answer to your specific questions, you may start to doubt your trust in that person. You might have a valid reason to wonder if this potential relationship is actually right for you. Consequently, you might want to delve deeper by asking further specific questions until you get tuned in to the person.

Questions are some of the best tools you possess to communicate in a deeper, more tuned in way with someone. We both like to use 'artfully vague questions', which gather in, like a fishing net, all sorts of information, and then follow these up with specific questions. If you allow yourself to be curious and trust yourself to ask more in-depth questions, you'll put yourself and the other person in a much better informed position.

Questions create understanding. We come from the angle that we want to help the other person understand their own reality even better and that through questions we can guide them. After all, they know their inner world more than anybody, and it's important they realise we accept this too. This acceptance creates credibility and trust. It's entirely possible you'll leave a meeting having said nothing about yourself yet having offered the other person greater insight into their reality. Remember the Trust Triangle – you can also decide if you need more time or want to talk to a third party about this person.

Be authentic

Be true to yourself.

What do we mean by that? Being authentic is about being who you truly are, showing yourself as 100% real. It's more than being pleasant to clients and behaving in a formal, albeit transparent, way. It's important that within a business relationship you can trust yourself to be authentic. You might be efficient, productive, and fantastic with figures and forecasts; you are also a whole person with a complete personality who responds to people and situations in various ways. You can be vulnerable, cheeky, sad, relaxed, scared – no matter what qualities and personality traits you possess, trust that you can let the world and the people you do business with see the different sides of you. Giving yourself permission to be the person you really are lets others know they can trust you. It's a two-way street because this helps other people show their authentic self when they're around you, socially and, more importantly, when doing business with you. Authenticity is a key to building total trust, which sits at the centre of our Trust Triangle. This is precisely how we acquire new clients in our businesses. They *tune in* to us and then subsequently buy into us and, if they decide not to, that's also part of the process. It eliminates any doubts, either way.

Work with people who share your values

You have to build or earn trust. A great way to do that is to tune in to people who have values that are similar to yours.

What do we mean by values?

Values drive who you are and how you behave in life. They are filters that help you decide which actions are right or wrong, good or bad. Our values are like magnets – they attract people who have similar values and can help repel people who have opposite values.

Values also drive behaviours. For example, if you cherish open, two-way communication, guess what behaviour that drives? We notice when a behaviour is present and we also notice when it's absent. From experience, we tend to be aware when another person's values are different from ours. If you approach every new person with the assumption that they communicate with an honest, open, two-way style, for example, it will become apparent through your filters or over a period of time whether they have the same values as you.

Values also change depending on the context – that is, we have different values for business, for family relationships, for friendships, etc. The most important thing to remember is to be true to your values, no matter what the context is. When you're completely tuned in, the other person's values can help you decide if you want to do business with them or somebody else. Your gut instinct guides your feelings about the other person's values and behaviours and tells you if you're compatible and can trust them.

In a trusted business relationship, it's important and desirable to have values which are compatible. How can you determine if the person you potentially want to conduct business with has the same values as you? Ask them questions. Find out what's important to them, what they like and dislike, and listen to their response before you frame your next question. As a result, you'll discover what you need to know and whether you can create a trusted relationship.

Sheila's story – the £40,000 lesson

Before the Trust Triangle had been developed as a working methodology, Sheila started a lending business using her own money. On the first few loans, the fees and interest were being paid, as expected.

One day, Sheila was approached by a potential client wishing to borrow money through her business and she tuned in by asking him numerous, searching questions about his life, his financial situation and the project he wished to borrow funds for. Part of the way through the process, Sheila noticed she was using her head more than intuitively tuning in to her gut. Her head was convincing her that he would be a good person to loan money to – he was seeking to refinance some of his investment properties. Sheila's head was saying, 'Yes! Do this!' However, the further she got into the questioning, into the understanding, into the communication about the loan and the details, the more her gut instinct was saying, 'No! Don't do this!' But…

Sheila ignored her gut instinct. Even at the eleventh hour, when she was about to transfer loan funds of £40,000, her gut was screaming out, 'Don't do this. No, no, no, keep hold of your money!' Convincing herself this would be a good deal for her business, she went ahead and loaned the money anyway.

Two years later, the client was declared bankrupt and Sheila never got a single penny of her £40,000 loan back, all because she'd ignored her gut instinct. Her only consolation at the time was that she'd lost her own money, rather than a client's.

In hindsight, Sheila realises that this loss was a positive investment in her personal and her business's development and growth. As a result of adding more rigorous systems and recognising good practice, Sheila's company, Sapphire Lending, was among the first in England to receive a full licence for lending from the Financial Conduct Authority (FCA). Furthermore, Sheila is in good company. She knows that business tycoons such as Lord Sugar, for example, use their gut instinct to make business decisions too. It was an extremely valuable lesson, and she's made that lost money work for her. The business has multiplied in value and attracted other business partners and loyal, happy customers who give us repeat business and know that trust is the new currency.

If you think that business is all about lending, then you missed the point. What it's really about is relationships, communication and trust – and it all starts with being tuned in.

3
Third Party

What do we mean by third party? In the context of this book, a third party is someone you already trust who refers you to another person or business. Or you might be the third party giving the referrals. Either way, third-party referrals help you create your trusted network, expand your business and attract new clients. In our experience, working with third-party referrals helps to speed up your personal growth and development, as well as your company's.

We'll demonstrate how the third-party element of our Trust Triangle, as shown in Chapter One, is strengthened by being tuned in to the people you conduct business with. Third-party referrals are also enhanced over time (the third corner of the Trust Triangle – see Chapter Four).

Defining third party

It's human nature to be interested in what other people are thinking about, and this also applies when we need to support a decision or buy products or services. When we trust someone, we also value their advice highly.

How does this work? For example, if you were seeking help in solving an IT problem, one of your trusted contacts might suggest you speak with a specialist with whom they've previously worked and of whom they speak favourably. Because you trust this third party, you can be confident that their recommendation is one you can trust. By tuning in to the person referred to you, you're able to build trust with them as well – to ask them probing questions and to discover if you have similar values. These are solid foundations on which to enter into a business agreement.

Some examples of how third-party referrals might arise:

- You're looking for something or someone – introductions and referrals to opportunities are given to you

- Someone is looking for what you could offer – people approach you first, unsolicited

- Out of the blue – you're introduced to opportunities that you hadn't thought of or explored, inspired by a third party

We were fortunate enough to be introduced to each other through a mutually trusted third party, who suggested we should work together in some capacity. At the time, Sheila was looking for a business partner and was referred to Fredrik. From Fredrik's point of view, it seemed Sheila was looking for a dealmaker for her business – and deal-making is an area that he excels in. We both like to work with people we trust. The honest, open, two-way communication and transparency between us has helped us complete several projects and reach a level of total trust we both enjoy. Working together gives us numerous mutual wins, including:

- Fun

- Complementary skills

- Aligned values (leading to personal and business growth)

- New opportunities and the ability to scale up

There have also been occasions when third parties we haven't even met have referred us to potential business opportunities based solely on our reputation and the way we work.

A third-party recommendation need not always result from a direct (or indirect) referral. We listen carefully to what people, whom we both trust, say about others. We note these endorsements since they may be useful for us to approach, either for business, support or as a potential opportunity. Listening to and taking advice from people we trust and respect enhances the whole likelihood that such recommendations are genuine and trustworthy. Our experience shows that the process of tuning in to third parties and building trust leads to positive and fruitful business relationships.

This was the case when one of the world's largest multinational technology companies was looking to commission a consultant who specialised in deal-making. Fredrik was recommended by one of the company's executives. It was agreed that they should meet and discuss the opportunity, and they were able to explore this potential relationship from a foundation of mutual trust. It was only a matter of time before the agreement was signed.

Online trust

Quite often, before we meet someone for the first time, we form an impression of what they might or might not be like, which can later be confirmed. Of course, in the digital age, there are endless opportunities to dig deeper for information without having to meet face-to-face initially. You might be looking for someone who can fill a gap, provide a service or become your next customer. You might also be interested to learn who, outside your network, is currently being recommended.

The advantage today is that it's possible to instantly search for information online about others. Your search may give rise to questions such as:

- Can I establish trust in this person?

- Can I verify what they say about themselves?

- Can I find third-party endorsements?

Content published online, from blogs to videos, websites, white papers, articles and podcasts, offers a starting point in your research to gather social proof about the reputation and trustworthiness of others. For example, they might share something personal in a blog or specialist knowledge which indicates they're a thought leader in a specific field. This type of information will create your first impression of a third party before you even meet.

You can do what is now normal and google someone and, as a result, you'll be directed to online resources such as LinkedIn, various websites, articles and news stories, YouTube videos and images. If your gut instinct feels right, act on it and make direct contact with the other person. This may be just the opportunity you're looking for.

Of course, others can do the same to discover information about you, your business and even your social life. If managed well, your online presence hopefully adds up to a trustworthy profile of you as a person, others may like to do business with. Therefore, it's important to consistently manage your online presence. If you fail to claim your own name, someone else will.

Referrals

A recommendation from a third party you already trust is more powerful than any facts, figures and research you might have collected. Good-quality referrals are the lifeblood of any business. The origin of a recommendation or referral is a happy customer; we both strive to base our businesses on doing the right thing, which leads to having happy, contented customers.

Fredrik really likes to give good-quality referrals. He does this by asking questions about what the person is looking for and then matching the information to the relevant connection in his network. Pre-qualifying people for this referral saves time for both parties. Say someone is looking for a broker. The broker can trust Fredrik to refer potential clients that may convert into serious and relevant business. This selective referral process demonstrates to the broker that his time and expertise are respected, and the likelihood of doing business together is far greater. It's important to use integrity when giving referrals.

Here's another example. You want to buy a new car. You might read several articles in industry magazines and various customer reviews on a make and model that interests you. However, if a trusted friend or relative then tells you about their experience with a different car they've just purchased, one they highly recommend, you're likely to consider a test drive in that car. In this example, we've shown you three different kinds of third-party information: the industry magazine, the customer review and the friend/relative, all of which might be valued differently depending on the context.

The power of third party

Someone else's recommendation of you is far more powerful than whatever you might say about yourself. A form of authentication or third-party validation is getting another independent person or organisation to confirm that whatever is said about you is true – that you are genuine and trustworthy. Examples of third-party validation include:

- Entering and winning (if you're lucky enough) industry-related awards is a great way to receive validation, and help to raise your profile. Winning awards means that you've been compared to peers and recognised for your achievements.

- Being introduced as a guest speaker by the host of an event positions you as someone worth listening to.

- Being connected by another person giving you a third-party referral in conversation usually means you're regarded highly.

- Securing testimonials, which are assets and position you and your business.

- Gaining certifications or trading memberships, which add to your business credibility.

- Achieving preferred-partner status, which means that you're already qualified and conducting repeat business with an organisation, and this implies that they're endorsing you.

- Being a preferred partner of one organisation gives you massive credibility (the power of association) when approaching other organisations.

- It is common practice in larger business transactions to do due diligence by carrying out more background searches and checks utilising third-party sources.

As humans, we want certainty that actions we're about to take are the right ones. For example, a new staff member is rarely taken on without references. Before you invest in your own knowledge or business growth, we suggest performing due diligence or background searches, and this includes gathering third-party thoughts and experiences. This is exactly how both Sapphire Lending and Sandvall Invest operate. We use internal processes and external third-party referrals prior to business and investments being conducted or brokered.

Over time, something new may well come onto your radar repeatedly, online or offline or out of the blue. It could be a person's name, a book, a course or an opportunity. Once your awareness has been raised, you become curious, and this often leads to further searches for information. Curiosity frequently leads people to the internet. Another way to get to know others is, of course, through introductions and referrals, which are the perfect example of third-party trust and the lifeblood of any business.

A third-party introduction

Mike, a trusted third party of Fredrik's, received an enquiry from John, one of his own trusted business associates. John, who was based in Dubai, wanted to invest in property in the UK. Mike's advice was this: 'You should really talk to Fredrik.'

Mike knew that Fredrik's property investment experience dated back to 1997, that he had built himself a reputation for his attention to detail, and that his highly profitable results spoke for themselves. He also knew that Fredrik's clients trusted him to handle deals and transactions from beginning to end. Therefore, when John asked Mike for a referral, Fredrik was the natural choice.

Similarly, John was able to ask Mike for a referral because he highly regarded and trusted him, and he was comfortable being introduced to Fredrik despite the fact he'd never met him. The subsequent twenty-minute phone call between Fredrik and John established that they shared similar values – and a military past – they had time frames that were compatible, and they took the same approach to control risk. On that basis they agreed to work together.

The result of this solid introduction enabled them both to build trust rapidly. Over the course of two emails, they were ready to commit to entering a binding contract. Fredrik delivered on his promise and, as a consequence, the original contract has been renewed several times since, even though the two have yet to meet. This business relationship benefited from total trust in the third party, as well as sharing similar values – which demonstrates that money follows trust.

4
Time

In this chapter, we want to share with you how investing time and communicating with people builds trust between all parties and how this trust can evolve into long-lasting, profitable and rewarding business relationships.

Communication

Thanks to the proliferation of numerous social media platforms, staying in touch and developing relationships with people is easier than ever. Over time, communication helps build trust and gradually, as you interact with certain people more often, they may be prompted to ask you questions about what you do, how you operate or if you can help them in some way. You might attend the same events or discover commonality in your past and backgrounds; these things encourage staying in touch while deepening your understanding of each other and building trust. Discovering how people prefer to be contacted (in person, online or over the phone, for example) shows that you've tuned in to their preferences, and this helps to cement the relationship. Different people like to be communicated with in different ways and within different time frames.

Time – allowing it, making it and embracing it – is an important commodity you have at your disposal for developing relationships and building trust with others whom you might eventually do business with. It's about growing the relationship. Start from a seed, nurture it until it turns into a giant oak, and enrich the relationship as you go so that it's fruitful.

Be sociable and open – it's more than just business

For both of us, most of our business results from being sociable with people we meet. As these relationships develop over time, trust is built. The more time we spend with certain people, the more comfortable they feel around us, which leads to deeper relationships and often to business. What we've observed is that people really engage with each other when they're being sociable. Connection and likability are foundations for any relationship. People like to see each other being who they truly are, which is more than just who they are when doing business. Naturally your core customers are usually the most loyal ones – they are your advocates. Our experience shows that trust leads to business and over time this translates into loyalty.

Being sociable usually leads to being open; openness equals transparency, and transparency ultimately leads to clarity. You can be transparent in your business life and your social life. Transparency is about choosing how much you're going to talk about the various facets of your life. Be transparent about any changes that are happening in your business because this transparency is as strong a benefit as the change itself – take your customers with you on that journey. Be transparent about your failures as well as your successes. Trust is never perfect. We're human after all. It's good to share how you overcame challenges and what you learned. Over time, the more transparent you are, the more likely your customers will reciprocate.

Be consistent

If you told someone you would do something, be that person today that you were when you made the commitment. Be that person the following day and keep that promise. Be reliable and demonstrate that reliability through consistency.

A trustworthy person is also flexible because situations can and do change. Circumstances in life might change between when you said you would do something and when it comes time to do it. We can all recognise the importance of adaptability. In the military, the commander gives an order and, more importantly, they communicate the intent and spirit behind the order. This allows the troops to act in the best way given the circumstances, and yet still follow orders and be consistent. Spirit and intent guide us to make the right and consistent choices in business. When situations change, adapt and be flexible in the new conditions. If the new conditions mean you have to say no to a client after you've previously said yes, be open and transparent and act with integrity. Keep your clients informed, which will maintain their trust.

Being consistent is also about managing expectations and being realistic about what you can achieve and by when. It's important never to overpromise, as raising expectations and then being unable to fulfil them will damage the trust that you've spent time building. Again, situations can, and will, change for any number of reasons.

Always make sure you mean what you say and say what you mean. Keep your word. This reinforces your integrity. Acting with integrity means never compromising your values. Do the right thing even if no one's watching.

Fairness and balance

Our subconscious mind tends to act like a bank account. You can deposit, as well as withdraw, small or large favours. A perceived positive is a deposit, while a perceived negative is a withdrawal. It's important to understand the intent behind a behaviour is as important as the deposit or withdrawal itself. Be aware of how you're perceived. Be mindful when depositing and withdrawing from a business relationship, as this relationship is ultimately about fairness and balance. If, over time, you've made many deposits and now want to make a withdrawal, the other party will see that you're being fair. Mutual trust allows both parties in the relationship to deposit and withdraw. Over time, fairness and balance are important in any relationship.

Lifetime relationships

Lifetime relationships are underpinned by trust built up over time, and they consistently show us that money follows trust. The higher the level of trust, the less friction and fewer obstacles will stand in the way of business.

We're both very much about building lifetime relationships with our clients. Rather than creating a huge customer base just for the sake of it, we work with clients who prefer to carry out profitable and repeat business. To build lifetime relationships, we start with building relationships using the fundamentals outlined in this book, and over time, total trust evolves. For us, lifetime relationships equal communication that's easier and business that flows faster.

Within Sapphire Lending, we build lifetime relationships through integrity, intent, delivering on promises, company values, trust and communication. All these things allow and motivate both lenders and borrowers to create repeat business. Often, as the quality of the relationship grows, so does the quantity of business. The lenders lend more, and the borrowers come back to us with bigger and better property development projects to borrow against.

In some lifetime relationships, trust in an individual is what's most important. For example, Fredrik has worked within several different consulting companies, and some customers followed him as he progressed from one company to another. In these cases, loyalty to Fredrik was stronger than loyalty to the individual businesses. In other lifetime relationships, the company itself supersedes the individuals within it. For example, Fredrik has developed a relationship with Apple. He's bought numerous products from the company for himself, his family and his businesses. The customer lifetime value from Apple's point of view is at least £20,000 to date and customer loyalty is worth even more than the money spent, especially as Fredrik has become an advocate and promoter of the brand.

The story of a relationship built over time

Sheila's approach to business is to be sociable, open and honest, and have fun in the process. For example, Sheila has a client that she first met socially, and over time, their relationship evolved into a real friendship. As the friendship and trust grew, they often asked each other, 'How can we work together?' Eventually, an opportunity naturally presented itself and they were able to strike their first deal together. Sheila funded a project for him through her business. This first project was successful, and it led to Sheila's business funding a stream of profitable projects for this client. The trust in the relationship between them has been built over time, and this allows an open exchange of thoughts when needed.

When you stay in touch with people you know and meet them in a variety of settings (both social and business), you allow them to see you as you truly are. We've found that doing good things in a consistent way, over time, creates customer loyalty, lifetime relationships and, most importantly, trust.

5
Total Trust

Our clients work with us from a base of total trust. Within Sapphire Lending, for example, we send lenders the details of new projects that borrowers wish to raise funds for. The lenders then decide if they want to loan their funds for that project. Total trust allows this process to be fast. At the core of the Trust Triangle (Chapter One) is total trust, which is held in place by three key elements – the cornerstones of building trust:

1. Tuned in – Tune in to yourself and your gut instinct. Once you do so, you'll be better able to tune in to others and make intuitive decisions.

2. Third party – A third party is someone you already trust who refers you to another person or business, or the other way around. Third-party

referrals enable you to expand your business network and bring you into contact with people you may not have previously known.

3. Time – Time is a precious resource we have at our disposal to facilitate building relationships and trust. Each of us can choose to use time in different ways. Time, used wisely, builds trust.

When you have all three cornerstones of the triangle in place, you can be confident you've built total trust, which sits at the centre of the Trust Triangle. Each corner of the triangle is both independent and interdependent.

Total trust is built from being tuned in, using third-party referrals and building relationships over time. Tune in to others, treat other people the way they want to be treated, ask good-quality questions and listen attentively. Invest time in building relationships through social interactions, as well as in business contexts, as this can lead to lifetime relationships, repeat business and total trust.

Trust is a business philosophy we've followed profitably in an economic climate where trust between financial institutions and their customers has been shaken up. For many established and emerging entrepreneurs running leading-edge businesses, trust really is the new currency.

Some of our guiding principles:

- The strongest relationships are based on trust

- When you trust someone, it shows you care about them

- An environment built on total trust offers people the freedom to be exactly who they are

- Mutual trust enables people to help and support each other

- Trust is the glue in any relationship

- Trust is linked to context – you can grant it in some circumstances and not in others (for example, you might trust someone to carry out a task in business, but you might not trust them with your life)

- Do business with people you know, like and trust

Habits

Habits define the way in which we behave and can be categorised by the words 'be' and 'do'. The following is a useful reminder of the main points we outline in Part One:

- Be

  - open, honest and transparent

  - authentic and who you truly are

  - reliable and consistent in your behaviours over time

- Do

  - act with integrity, keep your promises and meet your obligations

  - look out for other people's interests as well as your own

  - follow through on what you said you would do in the time you said you'd do it

Money follows trust

At a dinner party in the early years of Sheila's business, one of her guests, a good friend, was talking about a sum of money she had and what to do with it. She was aware of some of the options available to her. For example, she could leave the money in the bank and make virtually zero interest on it or put it directly into investment properties, which she had no interest in doing. An alternative option sat between the two, and that was to lend her money through Sheila's business, which would result in her receiving a fixed interest rate that was a lot higher than the bank's. This friend had known Sheila for many years and knew how her business worked – the total trust between them was already established. Within four days, the transaction had taken place and £50,000 had been loaned through the business. The matter had been accomplished entirely through total trust, and the transaction Sheila brokered for her friend was highly successful. Now, several years later, they continue to do business with each other on a regular basis. In addition, Sheila's friend has referred others to the business.

PART TWO
BUILDING THE BUSINESS ENGINE

In this second part, we'll describe the key people who create a powerful team that can really grow your business:

1. The trailblazer – a visionary and a go-getter, good at building the brand and creating and leading teams

2. The dealmaker – drives sales, does the deals, and takes care of customers and repeat business

3. The specialist – detail oriented, tactically looks at how to achieve goals, responsible for areas within their own expertise

4. The doer – gets the job, however large or small, done; produces results and satisfies the customer every time

6
The Business Engine

The Business Engine is comprised of three key roles in an organisation. These roles allow people to play to their strengths and create dynamic interaction and performance. The three key roles, the trailblazer, the dealmaker and the specialist, interact together and are interdependent on each other. The doers are at the heart of the business and are vital to the success of any venture.

The diagram of the Business Engine is also in the shape of a triangle. It's a simple, visual and effective way of thinking about the three cornerstones of your business. Populating your business with trailblazers, dealmakers and specialists ensures that you're covering all major areas of the business. Recognise the power of having a Business Engine and then build it – your business at that point will be ready to grow quickly and sustainably.

The Business Engine

As an entrepreneur, you'll probably identify with one of the three cornerstone positions. Or perhaps you're a doer. After determining which role you naturally fit into, set yourself the task of filling the other responsibilities in the triangle.

- The trailblazer will give you the vision

- The dealmaker will do the deals and take everything to market

- The specialist will think tactically and build your systems and processes to create the results you want

No matter which role in the Business Engine you identify with, the business will always start with you – the entrepreneur. What do you excel at? What are your natural skills and abilities? What are you passionate about? When you're clear on your strengths and understand your intrinsic role in the business, you'll be in a good position to fill the missing functions. You might already have people in your team who just need moving around, including yourself, so that each person is in their natural flow and brings their best energy to your business. You may, for example, be working as a specialist and yet your style, drive and energy is that of a dealmaker. You might currently fill the role of trailblazer when actually you excel as either a specialist or a dealmaker.

As an entrepreneur, you must recognise where you, and others, fit within your Business Engine. As your business idea grows, be prepared to replace yourself, if necessary, so you're free to excel, shine and thrive as the business owner.

Part of the process of selecting your team is based on the foundations of the Trust Triangle that we set out in Part One of this book. Once you have your key people in place and the team is working in flow, driven by their abilities while utilising their individual skills and capabilities, trust flows. The whole Business Engine is based on trust; everyone can be who they truly are because each person accepts everyone else. Remember, every person is different. A team made of different people with complementary expertise is a strong team.

For example, we automatically know – without any discussion needed – which team members' skills fulfil which roles in Sheila's business. This eliminates superfluous conversation and decision-making about who's best suited to do what's required. We flow together well because we know our own strengths and, just as importantly, the strengths of the others in the Business Engine.

Find the gap and fill it

We all have different strengths and weaknesses. By allowing people to play to their strengths, you can identify gaps and fill them. For example:

1. Finding the right place for yourself in your Business Engine is about identifying where you naturally fit in – what genuinely suits your characteristics, your skills and your abilities. Alternatively, you might think about which type of business suits you, your flow and your passion, or you may spot a role within an existing business in which you can thrive.

2. As an entrepreneur, know that it's always good to surround yourself with people who excel in the areas where you're lacking.

3. Attracting the right business partners is about knowing which roles in your Business Engine are available and, especially, who naturally excels in the roles you're looking to fill.

4. Integrating others into your team allows you to work *on* the business rather than *in* the business, so that you can focus more on high-level strategies for developing your business. Achieve this and you'll operate with the confidence that the business is growing without the need for you be too involved in the details.

Having selected an opportunity which suits your personality, skills and strengths, you'll be well placed to recruit the right people to surround yourself with. They could be trailblazers, dealmakers, specialists or doers. As you build your engine, the aim is to ensure each person is responsible for their own area of expertise – one person doing one thing, as opposed to one person doing everything.

Occasionally it is good to acknowledge that other people can perform better in particular functions than we do ourselves, thus allowing those people to fulfil specific roles in the business even more naturally than we do. Sometimes it's wise to step out of the role in which we excel and bring in somebody else who can outperform us.

Building a team moves the business forward. Playing to people's natural strengths means one plus one plus one equals more than three. It allows each person to shine in their distinct role. Taking action and doing what matters make all the difference to a business, which is why the Business Engine is comprised of a trailblazer, a dealmaker and a specialist, and has an abundance of doers at its heart.

In the following chapters, we'll explain each cornerstone of the Business Engine in more detail which, in turn, sets the foundation for Part Three: Partnering to Create Wealth through Business and Investments.

7
Trailblazer

A trailblazer is the light, the fire, the mover and shaker of a company. Trailblazers are drivers of brands. They are idea machines and people-focused leaders. Trailblazers can be the stars of a business and are often the public face of the company or brand with which their name is immediately associated. For example, Elon Musk is synonymous with Tesla. Similarly, Richard Branson and Virgin are, for many people, one and the same. A typical trailblazer's energy is high, and they're often described as inspiring, different in their thinking and innovative. Some trailblazers are outliers or disruptors, or both.

Outliers exist outside the mainstream. They naturally think and do things differently, and often in ways that oppose conventional thinking.

Disruptors change how we behave, how we think, how we do business and how we go about our day-to-day lives. A disruptor displaces an existing market, industry or technology by producing something new and more efficient and worthwhile (all disruptors are innovators, but not all innovators are disruptors). Disruptors can be destructive and creative at the same time. Rather than improving the status quo, a disruptor changes it. Take Uber, for example. They have disrupted and changed the transportation industry worldwide.

Trailblazers are excellent communicators and strong leaders who are passionate about building a brand. They love to create and grow relationships and lead teams, and they support team members to win and perform at a high level. Trailblazers naturally shine a light on the people in their teams and inspire them by drawing out their strengths. In doing so, they multiply and magnify both the potential and the opportunities created by the Business Engine. They always allow people to take credit for growing their own areas of expertise.

The way to attract a trailblazer to your business is to know and understand their characteristics and energy and ensure they have an environment and a role in which they can shine and blaze that trail.

The characteristics of a trailblazer

- They make a new track through wild country and guide others along it

- They discover, create or do something original and make it acceptable or popular

- They're pioneering in spirit; on the front line

- They're visionaries and innovative

- They often create new markets

- They tend to follow the rules less than others and make their own rules

- They rarely buy into what has worked in the past

- They're relentless and make perseverance a habit

- They take charge

- They're collaborative

- They're naturally trusting and build trusted relationships through helping people

- They empower others

- They give people the benefit of the doubt

- They build teams and surround themselves with people who know how to solve problems

- They make plans and overcome obstacles

- They have strength, courage and resilience

- They're dynamic

- They're optimistic

- They seek to understand individuals

- They apportion their success to the people who surround them – principally their team

- They see new opportunities and are ambitious and goal-oriented

- They're energetic and have strong drive

- They thrive on variety

- They build, lead and manage teams, and are motivated to do well working with and through their tribe

- They're great communicators and outward facing

Some trailblazers ask 'who?' while other trailblazers ask 'what if?'

The 'who' trailblazer

The 'who' trailblazer will naturally ask, 'Who do I (or we) know who can perform this specific role/task/ project/job?' They use their networks to find the right people. The 'who' trailblazer is, therefore, team focused.

We're sure you've come across a 'who' trailblazer, a leader and entrepreneur who understands that it's all about sourcing who can help with what. They know that the right people provide access to information and skills. Ask your team questions such as, 'Who is the best person in the industry to fix this problem?'

The 'what if' trailblazer

The 'what if' trailblazer thinks about the impossible and wonders how to make it possible. They typically ask questions such as, 'What if we could create and deliver this service in a better way?' or, 'What if we could give people a far better experience?' They're the creatives, the visionaries who sometimes find it difficult to communicate their vision to others because they're always moving on, quickly, to the next project. They're big-picture thinkers. They focus far more on creating ideas and products than on building and managing the team. Steve Jobs was all about vision and brand, and he found amazing ways to communicate these. Richard Branson is another 'what if' trailblazer.

Trailblazers tend to fall into one of three categories:

1. **The visionary:** Visionaries are naturally passionate and thrive in the role of creating the vision for a business or an industry. They excel in blue-sky thinking and create new ideas, repeatedly, at speed. Often, they're less capable

than other trailblazers at communicating these ideas effectively to their team members and the outside world. They may continue creating ideas before their previous ideas have been fully implemented.

2. **The brand builder:** Brand builders think on their feet. Simply by being who they are and utilising their personal magnetism, they build brands easily and intuitively. They're expressive, enjoy having fun and excel in presentations and performances.

3. **The team leader and team builder:** Team leaders and builders shine a light on others and use their excellent network of people. They energetically communicate a business vision to a wide audience, both inside and outside the business.

How can a trailblazer get the best out of a dealmaker?

- Give them a challenge

- Treat them with respect

- Give them space and autonomy

- Accept that they may choose to walk away from a deal

- Allow them to work on the deal itself rather than admin, reporting and other distracting tasks

How can a trailblazer get the best out of a specialist?

- Provide them with clear guidelines regarding the desired result

- Give them time to analyse and process data so they can arrive at definitive solutions

- Give them more than one thing to do (specialists love to multitask)

- Allow them to work in an environment with no distractions, so they can focus on what they do best

- Never micromanage them

The trailblazer is at the head of the Business Engine because their vision, passion and energy is what drives the business and the brand forward. They're determined and are prepared to take risks. They're leaders who can see a different future, and they set about turning dreams into reality.

8
Dealmaker

The typical dealmaker is a self-motivated and confident individual, highly energised and competitive, who thrives working with tight deadlines and responding to continuous stimulation. They embrace change, and when the status quo is shaken up, they often enjoy it. This fuels their adrenaline. They also welcome honest feedback, making them an invaluable asset to the team.

As an entrepreneur, you'll depend on a strong dealmaker to take an idea to market. In the early days of a fast-growing business, it's the dealmaker who gets the deal over the finishing line. The dealmaker is highly skilled at sealing the deals for the business. Clients and customers buy from people they like and trust, and these people are often dealmakers. The dealmaker knows that information, relationships and trust are the lifeblood of a great deal. The word 'sales' is synonymous with the word 'deals' to the dealmaker, whose main task is to find out what the customer wants and give it to them.

The way to attract a dealmaker is to offer them a challenge and opportunity to grow their knowledge, their network and the sales for the business.

The characteristics of a dealmaker

- They're curious – they find the best solutions by asking questions and constantly learning

- They gather knowledge and information and share the details of it at the right time with the right people

- They act with integrity, doing what they say they will, which helps cement trust in their relationships

- They have empathy – their natural interest in people means that they build their Trust Triangle quickly

- They have an ability to read and interpret others' non-verbal language, which allows them to instinctively take the right approach with people they meet

- They speak from experience and understand business in whatever sector they operate

- Many dealmakers leave their feelings and emotions at the door as they focus on the numbers and business in hand

- They are opportunity spotters and learn to focus their attention so that they can recognise targeted opportunities that can be converted into deals

- They know that timing is key in the deal process

- They are strongly motivated individuals with drive and an urge to proceed and, therefore, they do

- They have self-confidence and like to get things right and to get their own way, and doing so encourages them to push ahead

- They're winners who are driven by success – winning the deal is important to them

The advantages of working with a dealmaker

One of the main advantages is that they're action takers. They utilise resources, have good timing and maximise the power of networks. They also understand how to leverage money, which can be essential when making the right deal. Dealmakers strive to steer their conversations towards value and benefits instead of just costs and price. Their Trust Triangle strengthens as their deals progress.

Dealmakers work best when the finishing line is the main thing within their sights. It's important that they're free to work to their own time frames without having to consider day-to-day administrative tasks or look for extra resources required to help them secure a deal. Distractions such as these take away their valuable time and effort, which they'd rather invest into finalising a deal. Dealmakers drive to achieve excellence, which explains why highly successful companies all employ them as part of their Business Engine. They especially love rising to a challenge or seeing an opportunity through to completion: an opportunity that others might have passed over. They prosper on being part of a winning team and on working towards the success of the business. While they welcome praise and financial reward for their efforts, winning a deal is one of their strongest motivators. As well, their level of autonomy allows them the freedom to walk away from a deal when their gut feeling tells them that it's the right thing to do. For them, trusting their instincts – and knowing they're trusted in these circumstances – is essential. It's equally important for them to know that they're supported when a deal isn't completed (for whatever reason). However, they are by nature optimistic and highly driven and will quickly bounce back and enthusiastically look ahead to the next deal.

How the dealmaker relates to the Trust Triangle

A dealmaker uses all the Trust Triangle's elements – tuned in, third party and time, leading to total trust – to secure their deals. They understand that repeat business via an existing relationship, one that has evolved over time, saves effort. As a result, they create more deals with the same customer, and these deals often increase in size, which serves to make the collaboration even stronger. When you trust someone to share information, the space for a deeper understanding is opened, which facilitates total trust. This, in turn, allows the dealmaker to think outside the box, to consider what will be of maximum benefit to all parties involved. It's a route to creating the winning deal.

The dealmaker's relationship with other members of the Business Engine

Dealmakers are on the front line of any deal. They identify the people to engage with on both the buying side and the selling side. When an agreement needs completing, the dealmaker sets up a meeting between the decision-makers from both organisations so the contract can be signed. Meanwhile, the dealmaker is working alongside the specialists as they prepare the finer details and legal paperwork. The trailblazer, dealmaker and specialist rely on their relationships with each other to make business happen. Clear communication between the three key players in the Business Engine is of paramount importance. For a dealmaker, the outcome is often a successful deal due to their good communication styles and negotiating skills, their awareness of a particular situation and their ability to influence. In every case, the dealmaker is striving to help serve and to win. When the deal is won, they celebrate the success with the whole team.

The dealmaker is an essential part of your Business Engine and has an interdependent relationship with the trailblazer and the specialist. They coordinate deals from the outset by building trust (described in Part One) with potential leads, learning what the customer wants and then developing proposals that are relevant, or appealing, to the buyers. When necessary, the dealmaker manages time and engages everyone on the team to ensure that the deals progress. The dealmaker negotiates the terms of a deal and works towards its anticipated completion, and in so doing, takes ideas to market.

9
Specialist

Specialists are problem-solvers and experts in their field. They are highly skilled and have detailed, bespoke knowledge of a specific field, market, niche or area of activity. They can work with highly complex information and have a passion for knowledge. They learn quickly and thoroughly. They are talented, highly self-motivated and understand the big picture as well as the detail within their area of focus. They are analytical and organised in their thinking and able to keep a variety of projects on the go at once. Many specialists excel in maths, science and IT.

Specialists are often people who know how to bring the ideas and visions of a business to life through processes, systems, research, analysis and complex specialist information, which they make simple. They enjoy enhancing the vision of a business through their expertise and like to work harmoniously within a team. Generally, they are happy behind the scenes – building, analysing and processing systems, data and information – and their work drives the company forward and provides vital support. They are more risk-averse than trailblazers and dealmakers, unless they're working within their area of expertise. Following rules, policies and procedures while doing things by the book is important to them because they prefer to work with details and facts. Their honed, focused approach makes them efficient and effective.

The way to attract a specialist is to know exactly what specialism you need for your business and to ensure that you bring them in for the right reasons at the right time.

The characteristics of a specialist

- They can work with highly complex information
- They have a passion for knowledge and a thirst for continual learning
- Many of them are good at maths, science and IT
- They have an understanding of the big picture as well as the details of their niche

- They achieve tasks successfully

- They have bespoke knowledge

- They learn quickly and thoroughly

- They are highly self-motivated

- They are analytical and organised in their thinking

- They can easily multitask and keep a variety of tasks on the go at once

- They specialise deeply instead of broadly

- They have strong practical experience

Silicon Valley is populated with specialists, such as the technical engineers and coders who build the search engines and social networks we value so highly. For example, Sergey Brin, co-founder of Google, is a specialist in computer science; he's also been described as a mathematical genius. Jeff Bezos, founder and CEO of Amazon, is a specialist in computer science and electrical engineering.

Of course, specialists are to be found over many disciplines, across all business sectors and industries, from archaeology to zoology. Therefore, as an entrepreneur, you need to select the correct specialisms and appropriate specialists for your business. We often engage these specialists in our businesses: solicitors, accountants, IT people and project managers.

Conditions in which the specialist thrives

Within a business, specialists prefer being responsible for matters pertaining to their areas of expertise. They also like security and stability, and to do their best work, they need the right environment. They value being left to their own devices to work with no distractions, knowing where they fit within the business and how they contribute to the big picture. Specialists require clear guidelines and timelines. Being able to work on projects to a set timeframe and being given the space to deliver results are necessary for specialists to feel successful. They have a natural sense of loyalty to the team they work with or the business they work within. Outside recognition of their skills and achievements is also important to them.

Specialists like to stand out, and they respond well to challenges that allow them to use their specialised skills, abilities and knowledge to their best advantage. When you allow a specialist to shine, they'll achieve remarkable things. They also like to set challenges for themselves as part of their desire for self-improvement. A specialist knows that becoming an expert in something will offer them more opportunities to deploy their knowledge and know-how and to be publicly recognised in their field. Given their thirst for learning, the specialist will always strive to improve and will analyse how they previously achieved their results. Having done so, they'll produce something even better next time, rather like an athlete trying to beat their personal best. Environments with more competition will breed more specialists because of their wish to excel and their desire to test themselves.

A specialist is usually highly intelligent and often has a formal qualification that supports their niche area of interest. They are known for their direct communication style and reliability as well as their consistent (and persistent) approach to every new task. To the outside world, they often come across as quiet, yet their knowledge and expertise speak for themselves. When a specialist offers their considered opinion, listen to them. Their strength makes them a force in any business venture. They shine brightest when sharing their knowledge, and especially when they can create change in a business process or enhance the experience of the end user. They enjoy gaining a sharp, competitive edge for the businesses in which they operate, to make these businesses stand out from the crowd.

The right specialist with the right skill set at the right time is a highly valuable asset in your Business Engine. They will reciprocate your engaging them with their loyalty and trust. Engaging the wrong specialist with the wrong skill set at the wrong time will only serve to frustrate the specialist – they'll feel held back and unable to perform their role effectively.

Recruiting a specialist to your Business Engine requires careful consideration:

- Understand what types of specialists your Business Engine may be lacking

- Ask yourself if you can provide an environment that will allow them to shine (micromanaging them is unnecessary)

- Tell them who's driving the business vision, what the big picture is and how their specialist knowledge will contribute

- Be specific about what you want from them and allow them to deliver that

Even if you're a specialist, you may need other specialists to help your business grow, so that you can each focus on specific, and different, activities. Specialists offer in-depth knowledge, expertise and experience to a business, and through their ability and drive, they bring processes, information and systems alive. Their participation in a Business Engine creates sustainability and longevity. They are the heavyweights of any successful business, a key component of its growth, and will always overdeliver, no matter what's been asked of them. They have tremendous focus, discipline, drive and dedication. They give a lot and they expect a lot.

10
Doers

Doers sit at the heart of any successful organisation. They are equivalent to the worker bees who support the queen bee in the hive – without them, there's no honey. In a business, the doers are the ones who carry out the daily work and produce the honey, the results. This is why doers are the centre of the Business Engine; they work *in* the business, collaborating with and reporting to the key people in each corner of the triangle. All thriving companies have doers at the centre of their operations.

Who are the doers?

Starting a business from scratch is a time-consuming endeavour, especially if you're attempting to do everything yourself. Time, however, is a finite resource – there are only a certain number of things you can accomplish on your own in a particular time frame, so you need others to help your business grow. It's important to be clear on who's responsible for what. Building the right doers into the heart of your Business Engine is truly mutually beneficial. When you've done this, you'll jump the hurdle from being a lone entrepreneur or sole trader to a business owner. The doers in your organisation will free up your time and energy to scale the business.

Since no two people have the same educational experience and upbringing, each doer will bring different resources and skills to a business. If you attract the right doers to your business, it will be a joy for everyone to work together. Doers are pragmatic, hardworking individuals who enjoy the tasks at hand, and they pride themselves on accomplishing those tasks to a high standard. What might seem like rocket science to some is pure common sense to a doer. Again, this is why the doers sit at the heart of the Business Engine.

Understanding doers

Take time to discover, while recruiting and managing your doers, what motivates them in terms of working environments and benefits. If you invest this time, you'll be rewarded with hard work, results and total trust.

Some will prefer to work on bigger-picture aspects of the business. Others will want medium-sized tasks and others to concentrate on detail. No matter what level they operate on, doers enable strategic members of the Business Engine to grow the business in their own ways.

To identify the traits of doers, we use the DISC profiling system developed by William Moulton Marston in the first half of the twentieth century. DISC profiling is non-judgmental and helps people discuss their behavioural differences. For the purposes of our model, we've focused on three out of the four specific traits that a doer might have:

- Influence – they are expressive and energetic

- Steadiness – they are analytical and individualistic

- Consciousness – they are amiable and caring

The table below expands on these characteristics.

The characteristics of doers

Type

Energetic doer	Fast paced	Relationship oriented	Fun
Individualistic doer	Slow paced	Task oriented	Disciplined
Caring doer	Cooperative	Relationship oriented	Social

- The energetic doer likes to work at a fast pace, enjoys having fun, is relationship oriented, often thinks about high-level matters and is therefore less focused on detail and loves being praised.

- The individualistic doer likes to work at a slow pace and is disciplined, analytical and task oriented.

- The caring doer is relationship and family oriented, collaborative, sociable and likeable. They play to their strengths and are hardworking, loyal and supportive as the business grows.

Scale up your business with doers

As an entrepreneur, you must ensure certain things are in place to maintain trust between you and your suppliers and customers. The doers are an essential component of your business operations and can cover areas such as customer service, follow-up, retention, repeat orders, and both routine and specific administrative tasks. As you bring doers on board, welcome them and help them understand and operate within the company's values. If the right doers are taking care of the right things, you'll be able to focus your energy and enthusiasm on driving the business forward.

The doers give you the support to stand strong. They can handle small, medium or large tasks within the business operation, depending on what's needed. They're the oil that enables the Business Engine to run smoothly. You might have an appealing car, like a beautiful Bentley or Rolls-Royce, but – however beautiful it may be – without putting oil in the engine that car will sit on your drive with no movement. Similarly, your business can be appealing on the outside, with all its hopes and ambitions, its forward planning and cash-flow forecasts, and yet if it lacks doers at its heart, your business will pretty much stay where it is.

11

The Business Engine Summarised

We've described the key types of people in the Business Engine: the trailblazers, the dealmakers, the specialists and the doers, who are at the heart of this engine. We've shown how they're interdependent, play off each other's strengths and benefit from total trust.

Time

Time, as a key component of the Trust Triangle, is also very important. Everybody relates to and understands time in a different way. For example, a dealmaker's timing is essential, whereas to someone else, timing might be less important. Time is linked to managing expectations and to clarity regarding tasks and roles.

The Trust Triangle also shows that trusting your team enables your Business Engine to perform effectively. Harness the power of your people by understanding what drives and motivates them. Have clear goals and make sure everyone knows what needs to be done, and by when. Help people complete high-priority tasks and allow them to excel in their areas of expertise.

How to get the best out of the trailblazer

- Give them space for high level thinking and creating the vision

- Show appreciation of the energy they bring to the team

- Accept that they thrive on variety

- Work in a communicative way with them

- Join them in celebrating team success

How to get the best out of the dealmaker

- Give them a challenge

- Treat them with respect

- Allow them space and autonomy

- Accept that they may choose to walk away from a deal

- Allow them to work on the deal itself rather than on distracting tasks

How to get the best out of the specialist

- Allow them time to develop the best processes, systems and solutions, and time to analyse the data

- Provide them with clear guidance on the result that you want

- Assign them multiple tasks and substantial projects at the same time so they can rise to the challenge and excel in their own area of expertise

- Provide the right environment for them to work in – one with few distractions

- Praise and acknowledge their results and give them feedback with clarity

How to get the best out of the doer

- Accept that there are different types of doers and that they work in different ways

- Recognise and let them know that they are an invaluable part of the business

- When possible, create defined roles and responsibilities for each doer, which will allow them to focus

- Engage them in the bigger picture of the business and where it's going

- Match the right doer to the right task

Resist the temptation to hire people exactly like you

It's natural to be tempted to bring people into your business who are similar to you and to whom you can easily relate – people who think the same as you, who thrive under the same conditions as you, and who have the same skills and interests as you. Our advice is to think again.

The Business Engine exists for a reason. It's there to create balance and it encompasses all the major skills needed in any business. Remember, the triangle is the strongest structure – it's incapable of collapse. The Business Engine provides strength, reliability and scalability. Fill the three corners of your Business Engine with a trailblazer, a dealmaker and a specialist, and put doers at its heart to create a solid business model on which you can build and grow.

The aim of Part Two of this book has been to show you the right type of people for your Business Engine.

We've also shown you what these key people require to perform at their best. Remember, at the right time, you might look for someone who can perform your tasks even better than you can, as this will allow you to spend more effort driving the business forward.

We've also described how the Business Engine's trailblazer, dealmaker and specialist can work together symbiotically to complete the triangle. These relationships provide the business with balance, which is essential, and they will be as different as the individuals' personalities are.

The power of we

As humans, many of us are social beings that thrive on the energy of interacting, communicating and working with others, rather than in isolation. In our own businesses, we regard the people we work with as business partners as well as people we like to socialise with outside the business context. We operate as a team the whole time – we like to complete our projects together, win deals together and celebrate our successes together. This celebration fuels the team, and our playing together also deepens and strengthens the relationships between team members.

When your Business Engine is in place and working, you've used the Trust Triangle to build all your relationships within the business and with your customers, suppliers and partners, money will follow and flow. Our own Business Engine, based on the Trust Triangle model, continues to create opportunities for us and help everybody make money. It's all the evidence we need to support our business philosophy that trust is the new currency.

How Sheila built her Business Engine

Sheila is a trailblazer who's passionate about building and leading her team, developing lifelong relationships based on honest, open, two-way communication and trust, and achieving these things by actively connecting with, influencing and inspiring people. In some ways, Sheila is an outlier and a disrupter, and she noticed this especially when she entered the new and emerging industry of peer-to-peer lending. As a trailblazer, Sheila was in the right place at the right time; while the recession took hold, her business was born.

Sheila is often viewed by others as a disrupter because she doesn't comply with the norm – typical peer-to-peer lending companies are based on transacting via electronic platforms, yet Sheila's lending business is based on human communication, face-to-face. She develops relationships, makes connections and builds trust using the Trust Triangle (tuned in, third party and time), resulting in total trust between herself and her clients. Her business puts relationships at the heart of lending.

When Sheila started her company, she found herself filling a gap in the market. At the time, it was a wide-open space in an industry that didn't naturally fit her skills, abilities and passions. However, Sheila devoted a lot of energy to exploring this gap, expanding her knowledge and increasing her expertise so that, over time, she was able to thrive using her natural ability to connect with people and form new relationships.

Recognising that it would be difficult to achieve her business ambitions on her own, Sheila brought in specialist doers to carry out the work of an authorised regulated finance business. Knowing she was the trailblazer, she then set about getting third-party referrals to find the right dealmaker and specialist. Trailblazers like Sheila ask the question 'who?' – 'Who do you know who can help?' By being tuned in, Sheila allowed her gut instinct to guide her as she met various people who could potentially be the missing members of her Business Engine.

Over time, Sheila met the other two key players who were to become her business partners. They were attracted to Sheila as a partner because they saw her authenticity and transparency, and her drive and enthusiasm for the business. They had also seen the fun side of Sheila outside the business context. Sheila also saw them in different roles and environments during this process – building trust works both ways. Most importantly, her potential dealmaker and specialist were able to identify where they could contribute most to her business. Sheila's weaknesses were their strengths, and vice versa. Over time, one great specialist has been replaced with another for the next stage of growth.

All three partners work as a team and operate from a base of total trust. This is reflected in the fact that each person has the freedom to be exactly who they are. For example, they can be direct and assertive with each other, knowing that no one will take offence. They communicate freely and openly, and their different skills and expertise are celebrated and encouraged. The three-way partnership works really well because each person has total trust in the others; they know where everybody's strengths lie, what each person has to offer and who's responsible for the various tasks and activities.

Given the financial nature of Sheila's business, she's made it a priority to build a trusted team of doers who, in the main, are individualistic doers – analytical and detail oriented. They operate at the heart of the Business Engine, feeding into the specialist. Sheila's individualistic doers include a bookkeeper, an accountant, a data systems analyst and a solicitor.

As Sheila's Business Engine evolves and grows, she knows she'll attract other trailblazers who will be even better at some of the things she already shines at. This in turn will free Sheila up to work on the business even more, to keep blazing the trail, developing it further.

PART THREE
PARTNERING TO CREATE WEALTH THROUGH BUSINESS AND INVESTMENTS

In this third and final part, we'll introduce you to the Investment Triangle (purpose, people and project) to show you how important it is to have a win-win-win attitude (where both partners win and also other people or society as a whole).

12
The Investment Triangle

Now that you've built trust using the Trust Triangle (Part One) and attracted the three types of key players (the trailblazer, the dealmaker and the specialist) to your Business Engine (Part Two), it's time to bring everything together by partnering with others to create wealth through business and investments.

Purpose

At the top of the Investment Triangle is purpose, which is all about why you're undertaking/commissioning a particular project. When you have a crystal clear purpose that's greater than yourself, the people around you will be inspired; your purpose will guide everything else, bringing the project and the team together. A purpose shared by everyone involved from the beginning is your navigation tool. It's a shining beacon that will help you stay on track when things get tough, when deadlines change or when a different course of action is needed. It's important to return to and realign with your purpose – your big why – often. This will guide you through the challenging times and it sits prominently at the top of the Investment Triangle. Everything starts with purpose.

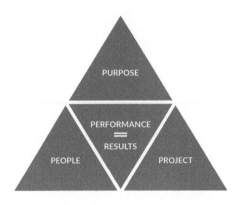

The Investment Triangle

People

People are a wonderful resource to help you achieve your desired results. There may be a range of people involved in your project, from stakeholders and business partners to financiers, specialists, suppliers, team members and managers. Each of these people or groups of people is an infinite resource for your business project. Leveraging other peoples' time, knowledge, money and connections will take your project to a higher level.

Project

Once your Business Engine is in place, your business will have projects that are key to its growth. Every project will be different; each one will run at a different pace, depend on different deadlines and timescales, involve different people, have a different 'why?' and produce a different result. You may have multiple projects going on at the same time, each running as a discrete entity. You may have a complex project which can be divided into smaller projects. These smaller projects may run sequentially or concurrently. There are many things to consider when planning and running projects in order to achieve the performance and results you desire. Projects in our businesses are often investments.

Performance

Right at the heart of the Investment Triangle sits the phrase 'Performance = Results'. Results are always agreed on by everyone involved at the beginning of a project. Performance sits firmly in the middle of the Investment Triangle because it's the combination of purpose, people and project. The Investment Triangle exists to create Oscar-winning performances and results for your business.

What's in it for your customers?

Without customers you have no business, so be clear about what you can offer them. It's vital to understand your customers' needs and their problems. Become a master of knowing what your customers' problems are and how they attempt to solve these for themselves. Determine how your business, your product or your service provides the solution to these problems by researching and becoming acutely aware of the questions your customers are asking themselves. For example, Sapphire Lending's customers, both lenders and borrowers, ask themselves different questions:

Lenders ask, 'How can I make my money work harder and better for me?'

Borrowers ask, 'How do I raise money quickly and relatively easily for my property developments and save time?'

Get to know the pain your customers go through in trying to solve their own problems and understand the mistakes they make. Ensure that your business offers them a well documented and well packaged solution that can absolutely deliver the answer to those problems. This is what will distinguish you from the competition.

When you're informed and understand your clients' problems and needs, you can truly help and serve your clients. In responding to clients' needs or problems, be articulate and precise – clearly outline how your solutions solve their problems. This will show that you've taken time to listen and understand their specific requirements.

You and your customers

Stay focused and clear on who your customers are, as it's impossible to serve everyone. Delve narrow and deep to determine exactly who your customers are – the people you enjoy working with and the people you can achieve a great result for. The important thing is to build trust between you and your customer, who will then entrust you with sensitive and important information, which in turn can help you to find the best solution. You must maintain that relationship with honest, open, two-way communication to continue building on that trust. There are several ways to show your customers you mean business and that you're worthy of their business:

- Thank them for their continued business and send them an email or note to that effect

- Follow up and check in with your customers regularly – ask if they're happy with the way things are progressing and find out if you can help in any other way

- Go the extra mile (ideally, in their shoes)

- Make your connections with your customers personal when appropriate

- Spread the word about customer successes

- Anticipate your customers' future needs – get to know them so well that you know when the time is right to offer more help

- Do the right thing

- Stay in touch – it's good practice, and you'll be front of mind next time they need your help

The win-win-win approach

This is an excellent way to create wealth through business and investments. Win-win-win is an approach to business that ensures all parties involved in a project discuss and agree on every aspect of it. A deep level of understanding about the needs and desires of each party is crucial to the success of this approach.

The advantage of win-win-win is that it builds a successful, supportive and cooperative culture around a project. The result is that everybody gets a 'prize', from the stakeholders to the project team and the business. It means that the project is delivered on time and within budget, and produces the results agreed upon and aspired to, from the outset. In many cases, there will be long-term benefits which outlast the project.

Partnering with people and strengthening relationships based on the foundations of trust will make the project happen. It's important to meet the expectations of all involved, so that every individual wins. For example, you might introduce two people you know – an easy action for you that can be invaluable to the other two people.

The beauty of the win-win-win approach is that it ensures relationships are built on total trust. Trusted relationships allow everyone to communicate openly and freely, and to focus on the issues of the project and its purpose. The flow from purpose to people to projects engenders many things, including direction, focus and determination, which results in better performance.

The relationships built in the win-win-win approach underpin our core belief that money follows trust and that trust is currency. In the following chapters, we'll go deeper into the individual elements we've introduced here and how the Investment Triangle draws upon them.

Here's an example of how we use the Investment Triangle in one of our businesses. We aspire to take a win-win-win approach for our customers and everybody involved. Sapphire Lending puts relationships at the heart of lending. We specialise in working with two distinct sets of clients:

1. Lending clients – people who have a sizable pot of money that they wish to put to work for them in a better way

2. Borrowing clients – property developers and business owners who wish to borrow funds to top up bank lending for a specific property project

Clients lending funds

The problem that lenders are facing is historically low interest rates from banks. They need alternative ways to maximise their funds with a good return in a relatively safe manner. The annual rate of return that Sapphire Lending offers is significantly higher than the rate the banks currently pay (and historically have paid). All the lenders who work with us have peace of mind while watching their capital grow instead of stagnating in a traditional savings account for which interest rates are lower than inflation (which means that, over time, they'll lose money). Through investing their capital, via us, into property projects and business, they increase their funds. All our lenders see a healthy return on their money, plus they get the initial capital back.

Clients borrowing funds

The problem that borrowers are facing is bank lending based on algorithms as opposed to relationships and history of borrowing. There are also lending inconsistencies across banks, and these are often coupled with slow decision-making. In addition, large deposits are frequently required.

Our borrowers tell us they can make more money for themselves, and more quickly, using Sapphire Lending.[2] This saves the borrower spending valuable time raising additional funds themselves and allows them to devote more time to their project. We're a niche business and we play to our strengths, so we can raise funds and provides access to them simply, easily and quickly.

There are many ways to broker deals, and our solution is the 5 Step Connection Method, which takes lenders and borrowers through a sequential process that matches the needs and requirements of both sides. The five steps ensure it's the right deal at the right time for the right person. There has to be 100% agreement from

---

2 Sapphire Lending Ltd is authorised and regulated by the Financial Conduct Authority. Firm reference number – 718266.

both sides. This method leads to trusted borrowing and lending and builds long-term relationships.

Ultimately, our clients and the people we work with are left feeling happy, satisfied and fulfilled knowing they've contributed to the UK economy and to society – they've played their part in providing much-needed high-quality homes.

13
Purpose

The *Oxford English Dictionary* defines purpose as 'the reason for which something is done or created or for which something exists'.[3] Many of us are taught when growing up that the only reason to do things is to get a reward. As we develop, we often forget the heart-driven things, the things we're passionate about. They frequently get left behind or forgotten because at specific points in time there seems to be no apparent reason for doing them.

What we do and why we do it can be broken down simply, as follows:

---

3   https://en.oxforddictionaries.com/definition/purpose

- What's the purpose that ultimately drives us? (the big why)

- Why do we carry out tasks and projects in certain ways to get the job done within a business?

In this chapter, we'll look at the distinctions between these two questions and how each feeds the other.

The big why

As human beings, we're constantly seeking to find a purpose in our lives and something to achieve for the greater or common good. In a business sense, for a project to be very successful and have a real impact, everybody involved needs to agree and be in alignment with its higher purpose – its big why.

A clear purpose sets high expectations, which lead to higher standards and better outcomes. Finding your why, your purpose, for the business or projects that you run is a process of discovery. When your why is clear, and greater than yourself, it will attract other people and resources to support and be part of it.

When everyone is aiming in the same direction, the best is brought out in all concerned because it's no longer about one person. However, we also believe it's important for all of us, especially entrepreneurs, to ask and answer these questions:

- What's your big why in your life?

- What's the big why in your business?

- Is your purpose something bigger than you which contributes to your happiness and feeling of fulfilment?

- Is your purpose something that lights you and your business up and gets you out of bed in the morning?

- Is your purpose something that you're passionate about, and when you communicate it to other people, do they also buy into it and want to make a difference in the world with you?

Neither of us is doing business just for the sake of doing business. These are questions we ask ourselves regularly, and the answers are what ultimately motivate us. Making our businesses happen is, of course, vital, and their success is what we constantly strive for, and that's because we each feel passionately about our individual bigger purpose.

Sheila's big why

My big why is to stop the neglect, cruelty and extinction of animals on the planet. One example of this is that I'm driven by my passion to do something to help some of the 100,000 stray and abandoned dogs in Britain that find themselves placed in rescue centres each year, through no fault of their own and often having suffered at the hands of humans. For years I've regularly walked some of these dogs at the local shelter, and they're wonderful creatures. They bring me so much joy and companionship.

I also deeply care about the men and women in the armed forces and our three emergency services. These individuals, on a daily basis, place their lives on the line to save ours – to make this country and the world a better place in which to live.

I believe there's incredible power at the intersection of these two causes, both of which profoundly move me. One of the charities my business supports and contributes to is Service Dogs UK. The charity takes rescue dogs from centres and retrains them to become companion dogs for veterans and emergency service workers who are suffering from post-traumatic stress disorder and, as a result, have been invalided out of the service. The charity simultaneously solves three problems:

1. The rescue dog is given a purpose, a forever home and companionship

2. The service veteran is given a reason to function (taking responsibility for and care of the dog), and this engenders the building of trust and closeness with another living creature

3. The families of the affected veterans begin to see their loved ones slowly coming back to life through the bond which forms between dog and veteran

I know that I can make a big difference by linking my business to two things I care passionately about. My clients indirectly help these charities and thereby also make a difference. Being able to contribute to a big why fuels and feeds so many people. It's a win-win-win. Contributing makes such a difference to me personally, giving a feeling of fulfilment and happiness. No longer is my business just about me; it's about something much deeper and more profound – my big why.

Fredrik's big why

Like Sheila, I'm driven by the things I'm passionate about. My big why is to help as many people as possible get greater control of their lives. I do this in scores of different ways, from public speaking and teaching to showing people how to work. During my time serving as an officer in the Swedish Armed Forces, I saw many ordinary people become physically and psychologically damaged as a result of conflict across the world. This experience has fed directly into my greater purpose, my big why.

I now use the experience, knowledge and understanding gained from my time in the armed forces to contribute to the greater good in the world. In 2010, the United Nations World Food Programme appointed me to set up the infrastructure and logistics to enable food delivery in the eastern Democratic Republic of the Congo, a vast country with few roads and tens of millions of people living without direct access to food.

We established an organisation that could provide and distribute food which was being produced in the Congo and the African continent. We knew that in the best of worlds, we'd need about 100, fully loaded, twelve-tonne trucks to distribute food 365 days a year to reach those people without access to it – amounting to a huge number of portions of food over the course of twelve months. To make this happen, I knew we'd need to pay our transport suppliers locally. I became a covert walking bank (which was extremely dangerous). On foot, I carried all the money needed for the whole project, in a territory where you could easily be killed for the sake of $100. You can imagine how much money I was carrying. I was used to dangerous situations as a result of my military career. My greatest fear wasn't for my health and welfare; rather, I was afraid I would lose the money, as this would stop the whole project. In my role, I was accountable for every single dollar. As long as the logistics worked, people would have access to food. Asking myself 'how many people can I help?' fed my own hunger. This is what drives me, helping others and fulfilling a purpose that's greater than daily business.

Seventeen goals to transform our world

On 25 September 2015, the 193 member states of the United Nations adopted a set of seventeen Sustainable Development Goals to end poverty, protect the planet and ensure prosperity for the world.[4] What we like about these goals is that they unite all countries and political and business leaders, including entrepreneurs, as a force for good. Entrepreneurs have great resources at hand and, together, we can create a better world for everyone.

Fredrik and his sons, Ivan and Charlie, focus on UN goal 4 – Quality Education. They educate others about different aspects of entrepreneurship and contribute to education projects around the globe. Fredrik is a strong believer that quality education plus action equals the end of poverty.

Sheila and her business contribute to UN goal 15 – Life on Land, which fits perfectly with her purpose, her big why.

---

4   See www.un.org/sustainabledevelopment/sustainable-development-goals

Fredrik and Sheila are both global partners of B1G1, which provides an easy way to make impacts around the world by making giving part of their business.[5]

The difference between motion and emotion

Motion involves behaviours and actions. Emotion, on the other hand, involves passion and meaning. Motion is behind *what* we do; emotion is behind *why* we do it (the big why). The why encompasses all the decision-making in the business or project, from the people you bring in to fill certain roles to the managing of the timelines and deadlines. You can change your what – in other words, the projects within your business – as you evolve and progress. Your why stays the same.

Microsoft is a good example of a company with a clear vision. In the company's early days, the vision was to see a PC on every person's desk – their big why. They believed a computer could help people be more productive and achieve greater things. Bill Gates looked at what computers could do and why the world needed them. He still solves problems in the world today through the Bill & Melinda Gates Foundation, which he and his wife set up.

---

5   See www.b1g1.com

Apple's slogan 'Think different' is their big why. It empowers individuals and at the same time challenges the status quo.

These examples show that it's never about what you do; it's about why you do it. Emotion is what drives you.

Agreeing on the purpose

Earlier in this chapter, we mentioned that it's important for everybody to agree on the why. This is a key element of making things happen. 'Chunking' (ie, breaking things into smaller bits) is a term commonly used in the computer world. Chunking up allows you to move from specific details to overall meaning – in other words to shift focus from the part to the whole. It also helps those involved find consensus at the level of generalisation. Chunking up to the level of purpose helps build bridges and allows agreement to spread across points of difference (people may want the same outcomes for a variety of reasons). Chunking down involves moving attention from the general towards the more specific (from the whole to a part). This process of chunking down, step by step, through the finer detail maintains overall agreement.

The specific why

Often there are deeper reasons why we do things. These deeper reasons drive us and are usually shared only with people we trust. When you know the real reason behind the why, it makes achieving the right result much easier. You'll need to drill down to find the specific why behind any idea.

Here's an example to illustrate this. Pretend you're a web designer and you've received a brief to create a company's website. The drilling down to the why might look like this:

Q: Why do you want to create a website?
A: To allow people to find us, to share information and to generate possibilities to sell our services.

Q: Why do you want to do that?
A: We want to strengthen the brand, connect to the global market and sell more.

Q: What will that give you?
A: Opportunity to expand the business and engage new people to join the Business Engine.

Q: What will your company gain from having those great people in the business?
A: It will allow people to work in specific functions and to specialise. It will also allow the business owner to delegate more and let go of tasks.

Q: What would that mean for the business owner?
A: The business can run without them, and that gives choices.

The final why reveals the real reason your client wants to create a website. Perhaps the owner wants the business to run without them because they'd like to have more freedom to enjoy other things in life – perhaps they want to sell the company or retire early. This was not in your brief.

Whatever the project you're involved with, specific questions can be a powerful tool to explore why the project is being considered. What drives us, our purpose, is massively important in the Investment Triangle.

Why disobey a military order?

This is a management lesson that Fredrik encountered during his military career in the 1990s. If you work in a military organisation, one of the first things you tend to realise is that if you're in a position of authority, you've got hundreds of years of history and a strict hierarchy to back you up. If you give an order, you expect it to be obeyed. In Sweden (Fredrik's homeland), however, the military operates slightly differently from the rest of the militaries in the world, and that's the result of one soldier asking 'why?'.

Normally, the soldier's questioning an order this way would have been viewed as a gross dereliction of duty, disobedience on a grand scale, even punishable. However, in this case, his question made sense. The order wasn't rational, and he wanted to understand why he was being asked to follow it. This questioning of orders became such common practice within the generation of soldiers growing up in the system that the framework on how to give an order changed across the whole army. Now, when an order is given, the reason why it's being given must be included.

What does this tell us? It tells us that asking 'why?' can help people move forward. If the answer to the why fails to add up, then it is, in Fredrik's opinion, perfectly fine to question that order. Throughout history, numerous crazy orders have been executed without any kind of sense check; if certain orders had been questioned, many tragedies could have been avoided. One 'why?' by a single soldier has led to thousands of people learning a new way to give orders – with intention and purpose.

Now consider this example in terms of delegation. Understanding why you're carrying out a task or action in a project, or asking someone else to, is key. In asking yourself 'why?' you might come up with a much better solution or encourage dialogue about the purpose of the task. The why (the purpose) is a gateway to greater cooperation for all involved in a business or project. Today, millennials (the aptly titled

Generation Y) are searching for the why more than any other generation. As entrepreneurs, we can all aim to use business as a force for good in the world.

Purpose, in our Investment Triangle, is about clarifying why you're running your business and what your higher purpose is. Freedom of choice is a strong motivator. In our joint experiences in the investment and entrepreneurship arenas, we've seen people progress from getting out of debt to supplementing their income, replacing their income, buying back time and then moving to a purpose that's far greater than themselves.

A purpose that's strong, unselfish and grand will attract resources of all kinds to your cause.

14
People

Without people, there is no business.

As we discussed in Part Two (Building the Business Engine), the people you attract to your projects are crucial to your business's overall performance. As your business scales up and becomes more successful, you'll work with many individuals outside your organisation. Then your projects, decisions and actions will affect a wider range of people, above and beyond those inside your Business Engine. As this chapter will show, external people play an important part in your business's success. These people could be:

- Business alliances and partners

- Sponsors

- Financial backers

- Connectors

- Project managers

Business alliances and partnerships

A business alliance is an arrangement between two or more organisations that decide to share resources in order to undertake a specific, mutually beneficial project. An alliance can dramatically improve the time it takes to achieve results and can also increase revenue. Partnerships can be long term, collaborative, value-creating relationships in which all parties benefit. If chosen strategically, they will enhance your brand and widen your reach. Expressed in a different way, $1 + 1 + 1 = >3$.

Business alliances and partnerships are based on trust. Crucial to any business partnership are good rapport, aligned expectations and shared values. Many businesses in the same sector form alliances and collaborate. For example, in 1997, Star Alliance became the first global aviation alliance, with five airlines. Today, twenty-eight airlines belong to the alliance. Each has their own culture and style of service and works in harmony with the others.[6] Alliances such as these offer unity, savings and, often, higher profits.

Alliances and partnerships also work across different industries. For example:

- Nespresso, the coffee company, partnered with George Clooney, the actor, to position their brand.

- Fredrik, an entrepreneur, partners with Simon Zutshi, who delivers Mastermind training in London, and Daniel Hill, whose company Multi-Let UK is linked to portfolio management. He also has alliances with property developers and finance providers.

Sponsors

Commercial sponsorship can bring a broad range of resources to a project and sponsors often look for synergy, goodwill and leverage to create mutual benefits. Business sponsors are most often linked to sports, as they want their brand to be associated with the traits of a high-achieving sports personality or the sport itself. They want to match winning and success with a cutting-edge or luxury brand. For example, Rolex is the official timepiece of Formula 1, and Audi is associated with many winter sports, which is a natural fit to its 4 x 4 ranges emphasising rural access

---

6   See www.staralliance.com/en/about

and freedom. Richard Branson has linked Virgin to a broad range of individuals, events, start-up companies and more, to reach a wider market.

As an entrepreneur, you may be considering sponsoring an event or person yourself. We've shown that tuning in to create your Trust Triangle (Part One) is essential. Tuning in to people and projects you might wish to sponsor is equally important.

Financial backers

A financial backer used to be a person or an institution that provided monetary support to businesses or projects. Now, the concept of financial backing includes peer-to-peer lending, private lenders, crowdfunding, venture capitalists and business angels, all of which are based on relationships that can be developed over time.

Warren Buffett is perhaps the world's best-known financial backer. He's famous for his ability to invest in companies at the right time via his business Berkshire Hathaway. It owns a variety of companies, such as Fruit of the Loom, and has minority holdings in Mars, Coca-Cola and American Express, to name a few. Since 1980, shares in Berkshire Hathaway have grown from $375 to more than $300,000 per share.[7] This is an

7   Figures from www.nasdaq.com

example of the power of compounding results over time.

No matter who financially backs your project, you need to ensure you're secure in your decision, and comfortable with your choice of backers, and that everything is in place with the right people to provide the results.

Connectors

Business is often driven by referrals from connections or connectors – people you trust. These people will have a different reach than you and can connect you to people who trust them, including those in their social network. Connectors can become ambassadors or introducers for you or your business, often out of their own goodwill by talking about or recommending you, and in doing so they also add value to their own networks. Similarly, you can become a goodwill connector for other entrepreneurs to create mutually beneficial relationships that result in business. The original connector usually multiplies the message of your business or project, which is essential to scaling. This relates to entering new markets and finding new staff, customers or resources. Perhaps the most influential connector today is Mark Zuckerberg, who, through Facebook, changed the way people connect via social media. Reid Hoffman – and the founding team behind LinkedIn – is another success story in terms of connecting people in business.

Project managers

Project managers can come from either inside or outside your business. Regardless of where they come from, they are people who display great communication skills and are able to share a vision and inspire a team. They are strong delegators and problem-solvers and, ideally, are very resourceful in terms of planning, organising, reporting and maintaining the budget. Tracking the project's progress and seeing it through to a successful completion, enhancing the collective performance of everyone involved and keeping the project cohesive are also responsibilities of a project manager. There are many similarities between project managers and orchestra conductors. Each section – strings, brass, woodwind and percussion – creates a different sound, yet the overall sound is that of a complete symphony. The conductor simultaneously conducts the rhythm for each section while paying attention to the overall tempo and flow of the concert. Conducting the separate sections and the variety of people involved in a project is the role of the project manager. It's about timing and rhythm, communication and organisation, planning, negotiating and leading.

Rapport

We are all unique. We each have our own fingerprints, our own DNA and our own filters through which we look at the world. Everyone is shaped by different upbringings, capabilities, experiences, beliefs and values, which leads to our unique interpretation of the world. Perception equals reality, and we all have different perceptions. No one is absolutely right or wrong. Understanding others' perspectives and priorities is key to succeeding as a leader.

When a diverse group of people are working towards an end result, rapport – and lots of it – is essential. Rapport is a harmonious understanding between individuals. It eases communication, helps us understand others' feelings and thoughts, and creates quality relationships. When these relationships are underpinned by trust, they become enduring. Rapport is like a dance between two people and can be built with anyone. It just takes time and a desire to see the world through the other person's eyes – through the other person's filters. You gain rapport by appreciating what others say even if you disagree with it. One way to appreciate what people express is to eliminate the word 'but' from your vocabulary. 'But' implies you've heard everything that's been said, but you have some objections, thereby negating everything that's just been expressed. This can be destructive. Replace 'but' with 'and' which is both innocent and inclusive.

Rapport relies on two-way communication. The observer must watch, listen to and tune in to the person speaking so that they can ask questions and take note of their language (for example, what words they like to use and what they mean by them). When you really listen, you create rapport. We engage, understand and connect, and bond with people to build rapport, totally trusting that the whole message we send out is in sync when body, mind, actions and words are all in alignment. This is an essential part of communication with others that allows us to be genuine and trustworthy. Smiling is also important, as it conveys optimism, energy and happiness, which are infectious and spread rapport. When you have rapport in a relationship, there is trust. When you have a trusting relationship, there is rapport.

We cannot not communicate

All our waking hours (and therefore all our working hours) we're communicating, with or without words. From the most basic and natural bodily function of breathing, to movements, gestures, facial expressions, tonality of voice, rhythm of speech, the way we accentuate certain phrases, all these things communicate our message – even words. Be aware that when you're awake, you're constantly communicating, either non-verbally or verbally. We cannot not communicate.

You may think you've communicated a message clearly to the people within your project, investment or business. However, you'll know if your message has been understood by the response you get. If it's one you weren't expecting, take responsibility for your communication and express your thoughts, your ideas, in a different way. Use alternative words preceded by, 'Let me express that in a different way', or, 'Let me make that clearer'. Alternatively, you could ask, 'Does that make sense?' Take time to listen to the answer. Sometimes it takes six or seven attempts before something you're communicating is understood in the way you mean it. Never give up – be patient and be flexible with your communication. We are all unique in the world and we have to take responsibility for our own communication to enable others to understand us. Once you're satisfied that the intention of your message has been understood, everyone involved will be in a good position to move forward together.

Two-way communication in the virtual world

If you work with people virtually, we recommend interspersing this virtual work with face-to-face interaction whenever possible. If you interact via technology with your colleagues and partners in separate offices or even countries, it's important to plan your virtual communication in advance, as if you were going to meet in person. It will help to:

1. Know the best time for meetings, which might require taking different time zones into account

2. Ensure people know which technology, tools or applications will be used and why

3. Know each person's preferred modes of communication (texting, instant messaging, phone, video or any other current forms of communication)

In this virtual communication space, how the data is shared is more important than it would be in a face-to-face interaction. Therefore, it's vital you engage, inspire, lead through example, and contribute by helping others and pulling your weight (as we mentioned in the section on fairness and balance in Chapter Four). In creating a plan for communication and carrying it out as agreed, you'll build and maintain trust. The person with the most flexibility has the greatest impact on the outcome. If you are flexible enough to use many ways to get your intention and message across to the other person then, as the most flexible communicator, you are bound to have a big impact on the outcome.

Be authentic and allow others to know what you do

The following is an example of trust and opportunity coinciding.

Fredrik was invisible online for many years due to his former career as an officer in the special forces of the Swedish marines. When he left the forces, he made a conscious decision to do the opposite and become very visible online. He now shows his authentic self by being consistent in his online presence, to allow people to find out what he stands for. This has brought him many interesting opportunities. Fredrik's frequent updates show him helping others and clearly demonstrate his career transition from being an officer (and a gentlemen) to an owner of multiple businesses.

Unbeknown to Fredrik, a former military colleague had been following him on social media for a number of years, and when the time was right, he reached out. They were already united through trust, having undertaken difficult tasks and dangerous missions together. This former colleague, like so many entrepreneurs, wanted to test an idea on someone trustworthy who could act as a sounding board. Fredrik's former colleague was searching for advice in the early days of founding a new company – an online trading platform. He was aware that the right business advice could multiply the results and growth of his business, ensuring an upward trajectory. He and Fredrik worked together on the business idea and soon formed a partnership. Less than eighteen months later, the business was worth ten times more.

What this story demonstrates is that there are people out there you can trust, and if you allow them to know what you're looking for and doing, they can help you grow and succeed. There are people who have walked the same path you're considering, so seek their advice – allow yourself to stand on the shoulders of giants. Why? Because you can. You probably already know who you'd like to speak to or work with, so there's nothing stopping you, apart from you. Dare to ask for help, which is exactly what Fredrik's former colleague did, and that led to connecting his business with a financial backer.

This role as advisor and dealmaker typifies Fredrik. He enables entrepreneurial growth and success in others. In many cases, the solution to a business challenge is partnering. Fredrik brings funding knowledge and connections and the investors bring their money, their networks and their experience. Fredrik's partnerships are possible due to the principles behind the Trust Triangle – being tuned in, having trusted third-party relationships and staying in touch over time, all of which create total trust. In Fredrik, the former colleague turned entrepreneur found someone who fitted into his Business Engine as a dealmaker (Part Two). Fredrik focuses on accelerating business growth this way, and his success has been repeated in many businesses.

15
Project

Projects can come in any shape or size you want or need, from creating a comprehensive brochure or website for your business to investing in a property to turn into flats for sale or rent. The success of any project is both objective and subjective at the same time – a small gain to one person could be a huge win to another.

How will you know when you've achieved the outcome you want for your project? It's important to be clear from the start what success will look and feel like to you. Therefore, at the beginning of the project, be aware of your success criteria and write them down. As the project moves forward, trust your intuition to inform you of how well it's progressing. You'll see for yourself what's happening, you'll hear what's being said and you'll have a gut feeling about whether it's moving towards the successful outcome you've planned for.

Timing and rhythm

In project management, a schedule is a list of activities and deliverables that each have a start point and a finish point. Between these are the key milestones which must be met in order to progress to the next stage. Linked to timing is a common tool called a Gantt chart, originally developed by Henry Gantt in 1910. It graphically illustrates how things are planned inside a project, usually in a linear order with tasks and sub-tasks. What's most valuable about this chart is that it shows how tasks depend on a specific order. It clarifies which jobs need to be completed before others can be initiated. You may find you have more time to complete the items in one part of the schedule, while elsewhere, the time frame is compressed, leading to a sense of urgency. A Gantt chart is an extremely useful, visual tool for any project. It will help you evaluate how the time within the project should be subdivided and how tasks and sub-tasks should be ordered.

Rhythm is essential to music; it's also essential to business. If you want your business to succeed, there needs to be a certain rhythm to what you do, when you do it and how you do it. It's all about timing, about producing strong, regular, repeated patterns.

No matter what the project, be it in business or investments, it will have a natural flow.

To establish timing and flow within your projects, you'll need to consider various things:

- Overall scope

- Timescales – what must take place daily, weekly, monthly and annually

- The actions and roles of each person in the project

- The frequency and nature of communication, reporting, updates, feedback and meetings

- The financial forecast, budget, cash flow, costs and the monitoring of these things

- The methods to be used

- The risks that need to be controlled

- How you will review the project and how lessons will be learned

- The time when a project ends

Ask yourself, 'What rhythms have I developed in my business or investment-related projects?' Remember, each of your projects may have smaller, discrete projects within them, and every project will have a natural flow, just as every business does. Find and establish your rhythm, develop it, communicate it, follow it, and remember that rhythm, unlike purpose, changes according to need. Everything has a natural rhythm and a flow to it: nature, our daily lives etc. Our businesses should follow suit.

Managing expectations

Managing expectations is about ensuring everyone involved in a project is clear on the desired outcomes. Specifically, managing expectations requires a detailed understanding of how and why you're doing things and continually updating all parties involved to make sure that expectations are being met at different levels. These levels include:

- Interpersonal – the relationship between the project managers and the customers can affect expectations, depending on how they're involved with each other.

- Technological – the technical aspects of a project can change due to variations in the technology itself.

- Situational – things *do* change, and when external things change, so can internal things, including the scope of a project and therefore the plans. This change can affect or shape a customer's expectations. It's rare that everything goes exactly to plan, so ensure you remain agile and able to adjust a project to the new situation.

Information gathering

Before any new project gets underway, ask yourself what information you need to gather in advance to enable you to plan. Naturally, this will depend on each individual project. In general, it's useful to consider the big picture as well as focusing on the details. Information gathering relates to decision-making and the actions that must be undertaken to bring an idea to fruition. Gather and consider all the necessary information in advance, and then ensure your team has everything they require to make your project run as smoothly as possible. After the project is over, turn your attention to the follow-up, which might include financial reports, lessons learned and celebrating the success with your team.

Measure what you manage

Information, facts and measurements make the management of anything easier. Gathering these things allows you to see trends and make better decisions. Most companies engage in continuous improvement processes to help them fine-tune products, services or business processes, resulting in more value for customers. When you measure your performance, it's much easier to understand what's going well or where change is required. A metric is a standard of measurement that helps to define performance, efficiency, progress, productivity, quality and processes. When measuring these things, you can begin to evaluate them and take necessary actions, which is key to any project. Metrics can help you build forecasting models and, in turn, improve resourcing, efficiency, productivity and decision-making. A project manager should be tasked with measuring and managing the progression of a project, including its costs, quality and time frame. Identify the problems before they become severe, so you can react and adjust early. Finally, at the end of a project, evaluate the completed work and results.

Measurements are important to link the progress of the people, the project and the performance. Remember to tune in to yourself as the project progresses and check that you're still aligned with your purpose.

In this chapter we've outlined the importance of timing and rhythm, managing expectations, information gathering and metrics. From our perspective, these four things are the foundation of all successful projects.

16
Performance = Results

At the centre of the Investment Triangle is the equation Performance = Results. Simply put, it means that the results you get boil down to the performance. To get the results you want, set up your business or project in the right way – employ a win-win-win approach, with everyone in agreement, and clarify the big why from the outset. This way, it will be easier to engage the team in your project. Everyone will purposefully work together. Throughout the project, ensure there is communication and everybody is informed. The flow of information will set high standards and yield great results.

When each person is performing as they agreed to, with boundaries, deadlines and rhythms set, your business and investments can only give you the results you desire and create the wealth you want. Paramount to all of this is trust. You and all the other members of the team must trust that everybody will do what they said they would do, in the way they agreed to do it, and within the parameters and timescales set. There has to be trust in the communication – trust that it is honest, open and two-way – and people need to receive necessary information in a timely manner to achieve their part in the project, business or investment.

Success comes in different shapes and sizes

The meaning of the word 'success' varies from person to person. Each member of the team will judge the success of the project based on how well they performed within the overall rhythm of the project.

When analysing metrics and results, it's important to remember that we're all unique – other people might look at the same data and assess it differently. Your financial backers may measure success by looking at figures, growth and market share, while your project manager may well quantify success in terms of whether the project is delivered on time and within budget. Your business partners may evaluate success in terms of synergies. If all the desired results are clearly agreed on at the outset and are achieved by the end of the project, then everyone involved can say, from their own perspective, that it was successful. Success, therefore, is about more than simply achieving a good financial result at the end of a project – it's also about how the whole project met the expectations outlined at the beginning.

Review

At the end of each project, it's important to take time to review the results you've achieved. This can be done as informally as you wish and should involve all the people who were part of the project. The review should happen shortly after the project has been completed, while it's still fresh in everybody's minds. Look at the project with hindsight and learn lessons for the future to ensure that everyone gets the greatest possible benefit and the best results. Ask yourself these questions:

- Is the performance what I wanted?

- Did I achieve the results that I desired?

- What worked well and why?

- What could be made better for the next time and how?

- Were there any unexpected results? If so, why did these come about and how did they add to the outcome of the project?

- What did I learn?

The insights gained from the review process will help you to plan future projects better and facilitate continuous improvement.

Celebrate your success

People who play together, stay together. It's easy to say, and yet, so few businesses do play together.

It's tempting to finish one project and move straight on to the next without taking time out to review and celebrate. It's essential to do so. Why? It's a great way to recognise what you and your team have accomplished together. Society relies on successful businesses to produce services and goods. Business creates the wealth that's taxed to fund our public services. We need healthy businesses and, within them, healthy people who are buzzing, excited, motivated, focused and driven. One way to make sure people stay healthy is to introduce some fun into your business, so celebrate your wins, however small. Stop, and then acknowledge, recognise and reward yourself for what you've just achieved with your team. They'll feel special, valued and appreciated for their contribution. Plus, socialising in an informal, non-business setting will further strengthen relationships, trust and appreciation of one other.

Instead of holding one large celebration at the end of a project, you could celebrate certain milestones as it progresses. Decide at the beginning of the project what mini-goals to celebrate and with whom you'll celebrate them. Milestones mark progress in the project. They're also opportunities to have some fun and social time with your team: time to renew and strengthen drive, passion, excitement and motivation for what's to come.

It's also important to celebrate with the people involved in your investment triangle as well as your customers. You might do so when launching a new product or range, opening new premises or supporting a charity event. Or you may want to celebrate a specific length of time you've been in business. You could also spread the word about your customers' successes. Whichever way you choose to celebrate, when you enjoy positive momentum from your accomplishments, this often sparks further energy within the business and ensures that success continues to be recognised.

Business partners – Sheila and Fredrik

Sheila

When I met Fredrik, my finance business had been running for seven years. In that time, it had grown organically, with one person doing everything – me. I knew I wanted to scale the business and felt the time was right to begin networking to find two business partners. Knowing myself well, I recognised that I was a trailblazer and understood my natural abilities and strengths. I knew the roles that I could automatically fill in my expanding business and at the same time was very aware of the roles that needed filling in my Business Engine – those of dealmaker and specialist.

I've always been an advocate of trust. All my life, I've trusted my instincts about people and opportunities. I also know from a personal development perspective that the more you listen to your gut instinct and the more you tune in and follow it, the more it will work for you and guide you. I therefore trusted the process of networking to help me attract the two people I needed to create my Business Engine. I was clear on, and knowledgeable about, the roles that every business needs. In fact, I'd studied these roles, their nuances and subtleties, in some depth, to determine exactly how to create a strong Business Engine. I'm a 'who' trailblazer and often ask myself, 'Who do I know who…?'

By asking people I already trusted, within a large network, 'Who do you know who…?', I was introduced to a variety of people who had the right profiles for my Business Engine. It was up to me to explore if we were a good match.

In communicating and sharing my business journey and vision with the people I met, I was open and honest, both as an entrepreneur and a human being. I talked about my values, beliefs, strengths and weaknesses. This was a matchmaking process. Then a third-party referrer I trusted and who knew I was looking for a dealmaker said to both Fredrik and me: 'You two ought to work together.' Fredrik and I tuned in to each other almost immediately and I appreciated his sense of humour. We started discussing how we might become business partners. Using this same process, I'd already filled the specialist role in my Business Engine.

Fredrik

When Sheila and I began discussing the potential of working together, as a dealmaker, I was thinking about and analysing it subconsciously. We certainly had complementary experiences, skills and interests. I know that I'm flexible when working with others and that I can work well with a strong trailblazer, like Sheila, when values are aligned. I admit that it's always flattering to be sought out and appreciated, especially when there is great rapport. I knew that working on a project together would likely be fun. I was also confident because the referral to Sheila had come from a person I highly respect. Trust ensured this whole connection process happened seamlessly and rapidly. Sheila and I quickly discovered we both have strong personalities and that we use our strengths in different ways. It was an exciting opportunity, so we welcomed the challenge of working together. What Sheila does is a bit like running a bank; she is focusing on the parts I find interesting, including making the deal possible by helping with the financing. There was a natural fit – I saw how I could add value and scale the business. The decision to become the dealmaker in Sheila's Business Engine was an easy one because the opportunity had all the parts of the Trust Triangle (Part One). Did Sheila and I want to work together, play together and win together? The answer was a definite yes.

Ticking the boxes

As an intuitive, tuned in trailblazer, Sheila knew that Fredrik was the right fit for her Business Engine. And as a dealmaker, Fredrik knew that working with Sheila would be a great opportunity.

Ticking the boxes – do we want to work together? Play together? Win together?

Trust Triangle	Trust in place	✓
Tuned in	Strong connection and rapport	✓
Third party	Third-party referral or testimonial	✓
Time	Timing was right – Fredrik had the capacity for what was required, and the time between meeting each other and doing business together was short as a result of the third-party introduction, which created trust	✓
Total trust	Yes	✓

(Continued)

Business Engine	Vacant relevant senior position and the chance to make a difference	✓
Trailblazer	Sheila	✓
Dealmaker	Someone who can focus on timing and who has specialist knowledge linked to the core business	✓
Specialist	On board a person Fredrik trusts who has entrepreneurial experience and specialist knowledge in finance	✓
Doers	No external staff at the time, a need to hire when turnover increases	✗
Investment Triangle	Clear potential, and in this case, 1 + 1 + 1 = >3 through many different synergies	✓
Purpose	Opportunity to grow and multiply the value	✓
People	Close fit with many connections	✓
Project	Very much linked to what Fredrik enjoys doing	✓
Performance	High growth potential	✓
Overall potential	Win-win-win	✓

We see the Investment Triangle as a crucial tool in ensuring success in business. Imagine the joy of having a clear direction for all involved and of having the right people doing the right things – things they enjoy doing – all in a strong framework with a start and a finish and, in many cases, an outcome, a result, which outlives the duration of the project. That's performance.

17
Conclusion

Trust is all about feeling. Either you have it or you don't, though this may change from context to context. In one situation you may fully trust someone and in another you may have doubts. When we trust a brand or organisation it's because we trust the people behind it. With total trust in place, business transactions are easier and faster – and money follows.

The foundations of trust

We've researched this fundamental topic and have found that when written about, it tends to be referred to in general terms. It's rarely discussed openly apart from when it's been broken or lost. By being more mindful and conscious of trust and understanding what it really is, you put yourself in a unique position. How, when and where you give your trust is for you to decide. You can increase the likelihood of being trusted by being aware of the promises you make and the behaviours and actions you display.

Trust has always been key to good relationships and, therefore, to how we conduct business. Trust is currency, and with your new understanding of it, you're now in a position to use this currency.

The Opportunity Triangle

The Opportunity Triangle allows you to pick and choose golden opportunities within your market. These can be narrow and deep or broad and general. The Opportunity Triangle is comprised of the Trust Triangle, the Business Engine and the Investment Triangle. They all work together to create opportunity.

In the context of business, opportunity is being able to pick great possibilities as a result of the right timing or set of circumstances. In a way, it's about creating your own luck. Entrepreneurship can be part of how you take charge of your future.

The Opportunity Triangle pulls together the three parts of this book and shows how they can work concurrently. Ultimately, when you have the Trust Triangle, the Business Engine and the Investment

Triangle in place, your business is in the best possible situation to expand. You can choose your position and your market. You can also create new markets if you want to.

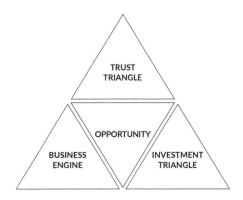

The Opportunity Triangle

Both of us have applied virtually everything we cover in this book to our businesses at different stages. When you spot an opportunity and decide to act upon it, use the component parts of the Opportunity Triangle to support your actions.

The team is everything

The right people, undertaking the right things, are essential to business growth. Trust is the glue that holds the Business Engine together. Honest self-reflection can help you understand your strengths so that you can see which of the three cornerstones are missing in your Business Engine. Are you a trailblazer, the person who has ideas, drive and the ability to make things happen? Or a dealmaker, the person who likes to sell and find timely solutions? You may be a specialist, someone highly skilled in a specific area (e.g., technology, law, finance). Doers are at the heart of every organisation. They bring speed to a business and they get things done. Your doers will have skills appropriate to your business.

Partnering to create wealth through business and investments

The Investment Triangle combines purpose, people and projects, and this combination will give you the results you desire.

Remember, there are two kinds of purpose. There's the specific purpose of a particular project (why it's being undertaken within your business) and the greater purpose (the big why) of your business, which is about using business for good – contributing to society or to a cause greater than yourself and your business.

The specific why keeps the team aligned. It empowers everyone to find their own unique way to contribute to the overall project and business goals. In our businesses, we want our teams to jointly agree on a purpose for each project.

The big why gives people the opportunity to support your greater purpose, which instantly builds connection and trust. It sets you apart from most entrepreneurs and businesses. When you have clarity mixed with passion, you become a magnet. This is a game changer.

Business alliances and partnerships are important to the growth of any company. A great approach to take is to treat all internal and external people, from suppliers to customers, as your partners. In Chapter Fourteen, we gave some examples of partnerships. In our businesses, partnering also includes introductions, investments and strategic direction from advisors and mentors.

Projects give a business momentum. They are focused and structured, with a start and an end date. You might also run smaller projects within a larger project (eg, a sales and marketing campaign).

A clear purpose and people who are aligned with, and contributing to, a project or series of projects will give you the results you desire.

We've written this book from a place of authenticity. There are many patterns visible when you analyse successful people and businesses. If you adopt the practices outlined in this book, you will, in our view, be far more likely to succeed. Without trust, it will be tough to run a business. You'll find it difficult to attract a team and clients and will ultimately be left on your own. In writing this book, we endeavour to bring trust to the forefront of your business agenda.

The Authors

Sheila Holt

Sheila's personality shines through in her business, which is unique in the finance sector as it specialises in building lifelong relationships, trust and communication. It's the finance business with heart. Sheila's lightness and brightness of  character together with her high energy, drive and passion take the serious and often overcomplicated business of finance and turn it into something that flows with ease and clarity.

Sheila recognises that she's both an outlier and a disrupter, which means that the standard career path never suited her – a discomfort which led her to a life-changing moment. Attending a neuro-linguistic programming (NLP) course in Hawaii opened her mind to entrepreneurship and gave her a completely different direction and purpose in life. Fascinated by how people think, Sheila developed a coaching practice utilising NLP to help her clients achieve clarity, focus and success. During this time Sheila was also actively investing in property. The big lesson she learned from building a sizable portfolio was that in the property industry money needs to flow.

In 2007, she loaned some of her own money to a property developer, recognising a need in the market. This was the first step to building what is now Sapphire Lending Ltd. The business has evolved and grown over the years and she's in the fortunate position of having attracted a great team, strong advisors and good systems. All this was accomplished by applying the theories, practices and actions outlined in this book.

Sheila has a postgraduate degree in careers counselling and an MA in research and education. She revels in being an entrepreneur and sees it as one of the greatest personal development journeys you can go on. She is a lifelong learner.

Find Sheila online at:

https://facebook.com/sheila.holt.9210

https://linkedin.com/in/sheilaholt007

https://instagram.com/sapphirelending

www.SapphireLending.com

Fredrik Sandvall

Throughout his life and career, Fredrik has focused on people and creating growth. His curiosity and competitiveness led him to become an officer in the special forces of the Swedish Marines. This role took him to many different parts of the world, helping others with tasks ranging from fighting organised crime to participating in diplomatic negotiations and working in war zones. He went on to graduate with an MBA from Lancaster University and used this to transition into consulting. His customers range from incubator start-ups to some of the largest companies in the world.

Fredrik is the managing director of Global Sales Consulting. In his role, he's a trusted advisor to entrepreneurs and business owners, helping them raise capital and win large deals. He's also a partner in Sandvall Invest, a family investment company which he runs with his brother. The company delivers excellent returns on cash and pension funds via ethical, safe and sound property investments.

Fredrik has involved his two sons, Ivan and Charlie, in Global Sales Consulting and the process of learning to become entrepreneurs. Together, they interview business leaders in the podcasts *Invest in You* and *Investing Skills*.

Find Fredrik online at:

- https://facebook.com/fredrik.sandvall.1 (personal)

  https:// facebook.com/FredrikinLondon (business)

- https://linkedin.com/in/sandvall

- https://instagram.com/entrepreneur4good

- *Invest in You* https://omny.fm/shows/invest-in-you

  Investing Skills https://anchor.fm/investing-skills

- @fredrikinlondon

- www.fundx.global

  www.fredriksandvall.com